SPECTRUM

ILLINOIS
Test Prep

5

Align
to Achieve
The Academic Standards e-Library

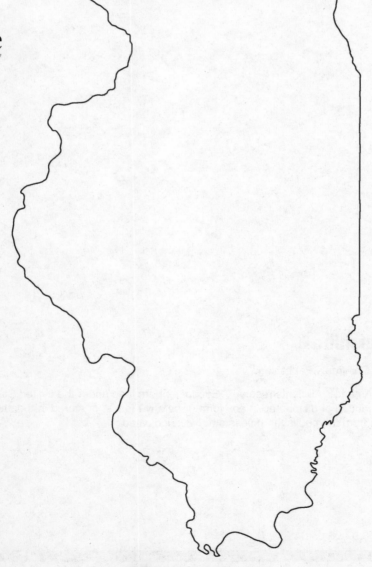

Mc Graw Hill **Children's Publishing**

Columbus, Ohio

Mc Graw Hill Children's Publishing

Send all inquiries to:
McGraw-Hill Children's Publishing
8787 Orion Place
Columbus, Ohio 43240

ISBN 0-7696-3485-0

2 3 4 5 6 7 8 9 10 PHXBK 09 08 07 06 05 04

The McGraw·Hill Companies

Table of Contents

What's Inside?

This workbook is designed to help you and your fifth grader understand what he or she will be expected to know on the Illinois fifth grade state tests. The state testing program measures student learning in different subject areas.

Practice Pages

The workbook is divided into a Reading section, a Writing section, and a Mathematics section. Each section has practice activities that have questions similar to those that will appear on the state tests. Students should use a pencil to fill in the correct answers and to complete any writing on these activities.

Illinois Content Standards

Before each practice section is a list of the state standards covered by that section. The shaded *What it means* sections will help to explain any information in the standards that might be unfamiliar.

Mini-Tests and Final Tests

Practice activities are grouped by state standard. When each group is completed, the student can move on to a mini-test that covers the material presented on those practice activities. After an entire set of standards and accompanying activities are completed, the student should take the final tests, which incorporate material from all the practice activities in that section.

Final Test Answer Sheet

The final tests have a separate answer sheet that mimics the style of the answer sheet the students will use on the state tests. The answer sheet appears at the end of each final test.

How Am I Doing?

The *How Am I Doing?* pages are designed to help students identify areas where they are proficient and areas where they still need more practice. Students can keep track of each of their mini-test scores on these pages.

Answer Key

Answers to all the practice activities, mini-tests, and final tests are listed by page number and appear at the end of the book.

Frequently Asked Questions

What kinds of information does my child have to know to pass the test?

The state of Illinois provides a list of the knowledge and skills that students are expected to master at each grade level. The practice activities in this workbook provide students with practice in each of these areas.

Are there special strategies or tips that will help my child do well?

The workbook provides sample questions that have content similar to that on the state tests. Test-taking tips are offered throughout the book.

How do I know what areas my child needs help in?

A special *How Am I Doing?* section will help you and your fifth grader evaluate progress. It will pinpoint areas where more work is needed as well as areas where your student excels.

Illinois Language Arts
Content Standards

The language arts section of the state test measures knowledge in three different areas.

1) Reading

Goal 1: Read with understanding and fluency.

Goal 2: Read and understand literature representative of various societies, eras, and ideas.

2) Writing

Goal 3: Write to communicate for a variety of purposes.

3) Listening and Communication

Goal 4: Listen and speak effectively in a variety of situations.

Goal 5: Use the language arts to acquire, assess, and communicate information.

Illinois Language Arts
Table of Contents

Reading Standards

Read with Understanding and Fluency

Goal 1: Read with understanding and fluency.

Learning Standard 1A—Students who meet the standard can apply word analysis and vocabulary skills to comprehend selections.

1.   Use a combination of word analysis and vocabulary strategies (e.g., word patterns, structural analyses) within context to identify unknown words. *(See page 8.)*

2.   Learn and use root words, prefixes, and suffixes to understand word meanings. *(See page 9.)*

3.   Use synonyms and antonyms to define words. *(See page 10.)*

4.   Use word origins to construct the meanings of new words. *(See page 11.)*

5.   Use root words and context to determine the denotative and connotative meanings of unknown words. *(See page 12.)*

6.   Determine the meaning of a word in context when the word has multiple meanings. *(See page 13.)*

7.   Identify and interpret common idioms, similes, analogies, and metaphors. *(See pages 14–15.)*

8.   Use additional resources (e.g., newspapers, interviews, technological resources) as applicable to clarify meanings of material. *(See page 16.)*

Learning Standard 1B *(See page 18.)*
Learning Standard 1C *(See page 34.)*

What it means:

Students should be able to use different strategies to help them determine the meaning of unfamiliar words.

● They should be able to use their knowledge of base words or root words to help them define unfamiliar words. For example, knowing the meaning of the word *reflect* will help them determine the meaning of the words *reflection* and *reflective*.

● They should be able to identify synonyms (words that mean the same) and antonyms (words with opposite meanings).

● They should understand that the *denotative* meaning of a word is its actual meaning, and the *connotative* meaning of a word is the positive or negative association brought about by the word.

● They should be able to identify and use figurative language. Figurative language is language used for descriptive effect. It describes or implies meaning, rather than directly stating it. Examples of figurative language include:

   similes—using *like* or *as* to compare things that may seem unlike each other. Example: Her smile was as dazzling as the sun.

   metaphors—comparing unlike things but without using *like* or *as*. Example: His body was a well-oiled machine.

   analogies—describing the similarity between things that are otherwise unlike each other. Example: The trees dress in bright gowns for the last celebration of the season.

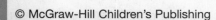

Reading
1A.1

Identifying Unknown Words

DIRECTIONS: Read the passage. Then define the terms that follow and write the sentences or phrases that helped you determine their meanings.

Budget

Always running out of money? Have no idea where your money goes? Saving for a special trip, activity, or object? If you answered yes to any of these questions, it is time to plan a budget and stick to it. Budgets have a bad rap as being too restrictive or too hard to follow. In reality, a budget can be very simple, and understanding how to use one can help you save for special things. There are three easy steps to follow.

The first step in building a livable budget is to record your spending habits. Look at your expenditures. Do you buy your lunch? Do you buy a soft drink or even water from a machine? You may discover you spend money foolishly. Buying a candy bar for $0.50 every day may seem insignificant, but by the end of the month, it adds up to $15.00. Instead, put a snack in your backpack.

The next step is determining your debits and credits. Look at what money comes in and what goes out. If you have determined your spending habits, you know what your debits are. Credits might be harder to determine if you do not have a job. Determine all the ways you get money. For example, count the dollars you earn or money given to you as presents. How much each week do you have available to spend? What are your sources of income? If you do not have a regular source of income, you need to find ways to make money. Do you have an allowance? Can you negotiate with your parents to raise your allowance? Offer to do more chores or special jobs that will increase your income. Check out the neighborhood. Lawn work and babysitting are two jobs that you might like. Remember, your debits should not be more than your credits.

The last step is determining your cash flow and savings goals. How much money do you have available each week to spend? You might budget a small cash flow for yourself because you want to save for a new pair of skis, which means you might earn $10.00 a week but only allow yourself to spend $3.00. Look at three important categories. How much money do you wish to save? How much money do you need for essentials? How much money do you want for frivolous activities? Determining the balance between savings goals and cash flow is an important decision for any budget.

1. **expenditures**

_____

_____

2. **debit**

_____

_____

3. **credit**

_____

_____

4. **cash flow**

_____

_____

Reading

1A.2

Word Meanings

DIRECTIONS: Choose the answer that means the same as the underlined part of the word.

1. care<u>less</u> thought<u>less</u>
   - (A) less than one
   - (B) full of
   - (C) without
   - (D) forward

2. <u>sub</u>way <u>sub</u>marine
   - (F) under
   - (G) over
   - (H) apart
   - (J) backward

3. <u>pre</u>arrange <u>pre</u>destined
   - (A) before
   - (B) after
   - (C) apart
   - (D) within

4. <u>un</u>happy <u>un</u>natural
   - (F) full of
   - (G) across
   - (H) false
   - (J) not

5. <u>co</u>operate <u>co</u>worker
   - (A) opposite of
   - (B) one
   - (C) together
   - (D) before

6. <u>mis</u>spell <u>mis</u>treat
   - (F) wrong
   - (G) beside
   - (H) correct
   - (J) not

7. <u>over</u>eat <u>over</u>spend
   - (A) without
   - (B) excessive
   - (C) into
   - (D) before

8. <u>de</u>frost <u>de</u>grease
   - (F) give up
   - (G) enter
   - (H) remove
   - (J) half

DIRECTIONS: Fill in the blank with a word or phrase that explains the meaning of the underlined part of the word.

9. <u>Re</u>play means to play _____ .

10. A <u>dis</u>honest person is one who is _____ honest.

11. Something that is treat<u>able</u> _____ treated.

12. An invent<u>or</u> is _____ invents.

13. Someone who is fool<u>ish</u> is _____ a fool.

14. A <u>post</u>game party is a party _____ the game.

STOP

Reading
1A.3

Synonyms and Antonyms

DIRECTIONS: Circle the correct word in each sentence.

1. We plan to visit Uncle Harry in one (week, weak).

2. Men's jackets are on (sail, sale) today.

3. An accident occurred at the track (meet, meat).

4. Cindy's papers (blew, blue) away in the wind.

Write three synonyms for each word.

5. pretty: _____ _____ _____

6. hot: _____ _____ _____

Write three antonyms for each word.

7. pretty: _____ _____ _____

8. hot: _____ _____ _____

DIRECTIONS: Fill in the circle next to the word that means the same or about the same as the underlined word.

9. successful <u>corporation</u>
   - Ⓐ business
   - Ⓑ team
   - Ⓒ person
   - Ⓓ country

10. skilled <u>laborer</u>
    - Ⓕ musician
    - Ⓖ professor
    - Ⓗ worker
    - Ⓙ relative

11. An <u>imaginary</u> story is _____ .
    - Ⓐ biographical
    - Ⓑ fictional
    - Ⓒ actual
    - Ⓓ humorous

DIRECTIONS: Fill in the circle next to the word that means the opposite of the underlined word.

12. <u>brief</u> description
    - Ⓕ important
    - Ⓖ lengthy
    - Ⓗ short
    - Ⓙ casual

13. <u>employ</u> the workers
    - Ⓐ befriend
    - Ⓑ manage
    - Ⓒ argue with
    - Ⓓ dismiss

14. <u>confident</u> in your abilities
    - Ⓕ uncertain
    - Ⓖ assured
    - Ⓗ proud
    - Ⓙ neglectful

Reading

1A.4

Word Origins

DIRECTIONS: Choose the best answer.

> **Example:**
>
> If *matin* means "early morning" in French, then which of these words probably means "a movie or performance held during the day"?
>
> (A) matinee
> (B) mattress
> (C) diplomat
> (D) matron   Answer: (A)

 Clue   Think of words that you already know to help you find the right answer.

1. If *mal* means "bad" in French, then which of these words describes someone who is not getting enough healthful food?

   (A) abnormal
   (B) malnourished
   (C) malpractice
   (D) formal

2. If *sombra* means "shade" in Spanish, then which of these words means "a hat with a wide brim to keep out the sun"?

   (F) somersault
   (G) someplace
   (H) umbrella
   (J) sombrero

3. If *vivere* means "to live" in French, then which of these words means "to bring back to life"?

   (A) arrive
   (B) vivid
   (C) vivacious
   (D) revive

4. If *graffiare* means "to scratch" or "to inscribe" in Italian, then which of these words means to write or draw on something that is in a public place?

   (F) graph
   (G) graffiti
   (H) telegraph
   (J) paragraph

5. If *dis* means "apart" in French, then which of these words means "to take apart"?

   (A) disassemble
   (B) discard
   (C) distance
   (D) disagree

STOP

Name _____   Date _____

Reading
1A.5

Read with
Understanding
and Fluency

Denotative and Connotative Meanings

The *denotative* meaning of a word is its actual meaning. The *connotative* meaning of a word is the positive or negative association that the word brings about.

Example: Mike *smirked* at me as he skated past.
or
Mike *grinned* at me as he skated past.

Smirked has a more negative connotation than *grinned*, although the denotative meaning of each word is very similar.

DIRECTIONS: Choose the word with the more positive connotative meaning to complete each of the sentences below.

1. Ben is good with his money; he is very _____ (cheap, thrifty).

2. Mikayla got a lot done as team leader because she was so _____ (energetic, pushy).

3. Jimmy's barbeque created a _____ (smell, stench) that filled the whole neighborhood.

4. The _____ (slender, scrawny) model smiled as the photographer snapped a few pictures.

DIRECTIONS: Choose the word with the more negative connotative meaning to complete each of the sentences below.

5. Asher is the most _____ (quiet, timid) boy in class.

6. The girls _____ (snickered, laughed) when I dropped the books I was carrying.

7. My uncle loves to _____ (talk, gossip) about the neighbors.

8. Melinda is so _____ (credulous, trusting); she will believe anything you tell her.

Reading

1A.6

Words With Multiple Meanings

Clue If you are not sure which answer is correct, eliminate answers you know are wrong and then take your best guess.

DIRECTIONS: Choose one word from the list that correctly completes both sentences.

1. **The player began to _____ .**
   Put the new _____ on the car.
   - (A) run
   - (B) fender
   - (C) weaken
   - (D) tire

2. **The sun _____ at 5:45 A.M.**
   A _____ grew beside the steps.
   - (F) appeared
   - (G) rose
   - (H) flower
   - (J) set

3. **My _____ is in the closet.**
   Add a new _____ of paint.
   - (A) hat
   - (B) color
   - (C) shirt
   - (D) coat

4. **Do you feel _____?**
   We get our water from a _____ .
   - (F) well
   - (G) good
   - (H) pipe
   - (J) sick

5. **Mrs. Johnson said Carrie was a _____ student.**
   The light from the headlights was _____ .
   - (A) noisy
   - (B) red
   - (C) bright
   - (D) hard working

DIRECTIONS: Choose the answer that uses the underlined word from the example in the same way.

6. **Please <u>file</u> these papers.**
   - (F) The counselor pulled out her file on the Jones family.
   - (G) Sally used a file to smooth her fingernails.
   - (H) I put the file cards in order.
   - (J) Jane asked her secretary to file the reports on water safety.

7. **I used a <u>lemon</u> to make lemonade.**
   - (A) The color of the baby's room is lemon.
   - (B) That car was a lemon.
   - (C) This cleaner has a lovely lemon scent.
   - (D) Rachel bought a lemon at the store.

Figurative Language

DIRECTIONS: Read the passage and then match each idiom with its meaning.

Food for Thought

A waiter was taking a break. He said to a brand new employee, "You just have to be the one <u>to break the ice</u> with the chef. Sometimes it seems like he has <u>a chip on his shoulder</u>, but he's okay. This is a busy place. You've jumped <u>out of the frying pan and into the fire</u>, let me tell you. I hope you don't have any <u>pie-in-the-sky</u> ideas about taking things easy here. Some days, I feel like I'm <u>going bananas</u>. It might not be your <u>cup of tea</u>. I think we've got <u>the cream of the crop</u> here; everybody does a great job. It's hard sometimes not to <u>fly off the handle</u> when things are so hectic, though. I think you'll do all right if you don't mind hard work."

1. _____ to break the ice

2. _____ a chip on his shoulder

3. _____ out of the frying pan and into the fire

4. _____ pie-in-the-sky

5. _____ going bananas

6. _____ cup of tea

7. _____ the cream of the crop

8. _____ fly off the handle

A unrealistic

B something one enjoys

C the best available

D to make a start

E to lose one's temper

F seemingly angry or resentful

G go crazy

H from a bad situation to a worse one

STOP

Reading

1A.7

Figurative Language

DIRECTIONS: Read the passage and answer the questions that follow.

Autumn Dance

Every October, autumn bullies summer into letting go of the skies. The wind breathes a chill into the air. The sun gets tired and goes to bed earlier each night, and night sleeps in later each day. The trees dress in bright gowns for the last celebration of the season, and the leaves are skipping and dancing down the sidewalk. This is autumn, standing firm with hands on her hips, until winter peers over the edge of the world.

1. This passage tells about _____ .

   (A) winter turning into spring

   (B) fall turning into winter

   (C) spring turning into summer

   (D) summer turning into fall

2. How does the sun change during autumn?

   (F) It rises and sets earlier than in the summer.

   (G) It rises and sets later than in the summer.

   (H) It rises later but sets earlier than in the summer.

   (J) It rises earlier but sets later than in the summer.

3. What is the author referring to when she describes the trees dressed in "bright gowns"?

   (A) leaves that have changed color but have not yet fallen from the trees

   (B) green leaves

   (C) formal dresses

   (D) the trees' empty branches

4. An analogy is a similarity between things that are otherwise unlike each other. In the passage, an analogy is being made between the trees and _____ .

   (F) boys playing football

   (G) girls going to a party

   (H) boys riding a merry-go-round

   (J) girls swimming in a pool

5. A simile is a figure of speech comparing two unlike things. Which simile is implied in this passage?

   (A) The autumn sun is like a sleepy child.

   (B) The autumn leaves are like sleepy children.

   (C) The autumn wind is like a sleepy child.

   (D) The autumn trees are like sleepy children.

STOP

Reading

1A.8

Clarifying Meanings with Additional Resources

Read with Understanding and Fluency

DIRECTIONS: Use the dictionary entries to answer questions 1–3.

save [sāv] *v.* **1.** to rescue from harm or danger. **2.** to keep in a safe condition. **3.** to set aside for future use; store. **4.** to avoid.

saving [sā´vĭng] *n.* **1.** rescuing from harm or danger. **2.** avoiding excess spending; economy. **3.** something saved.

savory [sā´və-rē] *adj.* **1.** appealing to the taste or smell. **2.** salty to the taste.

1. **The *a* in the word *saving* sounds most like the word _____.**
   - (A) pat
   - (B) ape
   - (C) heated
   - (D) naughty

2. **Which sentence uses *save* in the same way as definition number 3?**
   - (F) Firefighters save lives.
   - (G) She saves half of all she earns.
   - (H) Going by jet saves eight hours of driving.
   - (J) The life jacket saved the boy from drowning.

3. **Which sentence uses *savory* in the same way as definition number 2?**
   - (A) The savory stew made me thirsty.
   - (B) The savory bank opened an account.
   - (C) This flower has a savory scent.
   - (D) The savory dog rescued me.

DIRECTIONS: Use the dictionary entry to answer questions 4 and 5.

beam [bēm] *n.* **1.** a squared-off log used to support a building. **2.** a ray of light. **3.** the wooden roller in a loom. *v.* **1.** to shine. **2.** to smile broadly.

4. **Which sentence uses the word *beam* in the same way as the first definition of the noun?**
   - (F) The beam held up the plaster ceiling.
   - (G) The beam of sunlight warmed the room.
   - (H) She moved the beam before she added a row of wool.
   - (J) The bright stars beam in the night sky.

5. **Which sentence uses the word *beam* in the same way as the third definition of the noun?**
   - (A) The ceiling beam had fallen into the room.
   - (B) She moved the beam before she added a row of wool.
   - (C) She beamed her approval.
   - (D) The beam of sunlight came through the tree.

STOP

Reading

1A

For pages 8–16

Mini-Test 1

DIRECTIONS: Choose the word that correctly completes both sentences.

1. Someone bought the _____ on the corner.
   A new house costs a _____ of money.
   - (A) bunch
   - (B) lot
   - (C) house
   - (D) property

2. Inez bought a _____ of soda.
   The doctor said it was a difficult _____ .
   - (F) case
   - (G) carton
   - (H) disease
   - (J) situation

DIRECTIONS: Fill in the circle next to the word that means the same or about the same as the underlined word.

3. Complete the <u>assignment</u>.
   - (A) task
   - (B) assistant
   - (C) design
   - (D) office

4. <u>Focus</u> your attention.
   - (F) fluctuate
   - (G) irritate
   - (H) compile
   - (J) concentrate

DIRECTIONS: Fill in the circle next to the word that means the opposite of the underlined word.

5. <u>express</u> your thoughts
   - (A) yell
   - (B) withhold
   - (C) summarize
   - (D) tell

6. <u>obvious</u> signs
   - (F) unclear
   - (G) apparent
   - (H) momentary
   - (J) secondary

DIRECTIONS: Fill in the circle next to the sentence that contains a simile.

7.
   - (A) The sunset was a beautiful rainbow of color.
   - (B) He was hungry enough to eat an elephant.
   - (C) Sasha's memories were like the pages of a book.
   - (D) The light flickered and then went out.

DIRECTIONS: Choose the answer that means the same as the underlined part of the words.

8. <u>re</u>apply <u>re</u>arrange
   - (F) opposite of
   - (G) full of
   - (H) again
   - (J) forward

9. <u>over</u>do <u>over</u>cook
   - (A) excessive
   - (B) without
   - (C) into
   - (D) before

Reading Standards

Read with Understanding and Fluency

Goal 1: Read with understanding and fluency.

Learning Standard 1A *(See page 7.)*

Learning Standard 1B—Students who meet the standard can apply reading strategies to improve understanding and fluency.

1. Set a purpose for reading and adjust as necessary before and during reading. *(See page 19.)*
2. Formulate questions to determine meaning based on plot, character, action, or setting. *(See page 20.)*
3. Apply survey strategies (e.g., use of bold print, organization of content, key words, graphics). *(See pages 21–22.)*
4. Make judgments based on prior knowledge during reading. *(See page 23.)*
5. Distinguish between significant and minor details. *(See pages 24–25.)*
6. Connect, clarify, and extend ideas through discussions, activities, and various classroom groupings (e.g., partners, small group, ability levels, interest levels). *(See pages 26–27.)*
7. Identify structure (e.g., description, compare, cause/effect, sequence) of nonfiction text to improve comprehension. *(See pages 28–29.)*
8. Demonstrate understanding of structure through the use of graphic organizers and outlining (e.g., mapping, time lines, Venn diagrams). *(See pages 30–31.)*

What it means:
- Students should be able to recognize that literature from different periods of history and from different cultures follow similar patterns and have common characteristics.

9. Apply self-monitoring and self-correcting strategies (e.g., reread, read ahead, use visual and context clues, ask questions, retell, clarify terminology, seek additional information) continuously to clarify understanding during reading. *(See page 32.)*
10. Read age-appropriate material aloud with fluency and accuracy.

Learning Standard 1C *(See page 34.)*

Setting a Purpose for Reading

DIRECTIONS: Before you read the passage below, read the questions first. Now read the passage, adjusting your strategies as needed to answer the questions.

> Today was very busy. Jane, Carl, and I went out around 8:00 to fill our buckets with blackberries. It was hard work, and we didn't get back until it was time for lunch. This afternoon, Aunt Mara showed us how to wash and sort the berries. When it was time to make jam, Aunt Mara did the cooking part. Then she let us fill the jars and decorate the labels. Now Aunt Mara is letting me take a jar of jam home for Mom. She'll be surprised that I helped make it. I hope the rest of my stay here is as much fun as today was.

1. **What was the first thing the narrator did?**
   - (A) picked blackberries
   - (B) ate lunch
   - (C) decorated labels
   - (D) washed berries

2. **Who cooked the berries?**
   - (F) the narrator
   - (G) Jane
   - (H) Carl
   - (J) Aunt Mara

3. **How does the narrator feel about this experience?**
   - (A) frustrated
   - (B) surprised
   - (C) happy
   - (D) angry

4. **When did the children pick the berries?**
   - (F) at night
   - (G) in the afternoon
   - (H) in the evening
   - (J) in the morning

5. **What did Aunt Mara do when they were making the jam?**
   - (A) She washed the berries.
   - (B) She filled the jars.
   - (C) She decorated the labels.
   - (D) She cooked the berries.

6. **Approximately how long did it take to pick the berries?**
   - (F) two hours
   - (G) three hours
   - (H) four hours
   - (J) all day

STOP

Name _____ Date _____

Reading

1B.2

Read with
Understanding
and Fluency

Asking Questions to Determine Meaning

DIRECTIONS: Read the passage and answer the following questions.

Clue

Asking questions as you read can help you determine the meaning of the passage.

The Race Is On!

Lee and Kim are both running for class president. This is a big job. The president has to help organize special events for the class, such as environmental projects, holiday parties, visit-the-elderly outings, and field trips.

Lee has been campaigning for several weeks. He really wants to be elected president. He prepared a speech telling the class all of the great ideas he hopes to accomplish if he wins. For example, Lee wants to have a car wash and picnic to earn money for the homeless. He also wants to recycle aluminum cans to earn money for a field trip to the new Exploration Science Center. Lee has been working hard for this position.

Kim hasn't done much, if any, campaigning. She figures she has lots of friends who will vote for her. Instead of a speech, she gave a big pool party at her house. Kim believes the class should work to earn money, but she believes that any money they raise should be used for their class. Why give money to someone else when there are lots of great places to visit on field trips in their city?

The day of the big election arrives. The votes are in. The winner is . . .

1. **Which of the following questions might help you determine the meaning of this passage?**

    (A) What grade are Lee and Kim in?

    (B) Who seems to have worked the hardest to be elected?

    (C) How much money does Kim hope to raise for her class?

    (D) How old is Lee?

2. **Which of the following questions will not help you determine the meaning of this passage?**

    (F) What are Lee and Kim's campaign tactics?

    (G) Why has Kim not done much campaigning?

    (H) How old is Lee?

    (J) Who seems to have worked the hardest to be elected?

STOP

Applying Survey Strategies

A Delicious Dinner

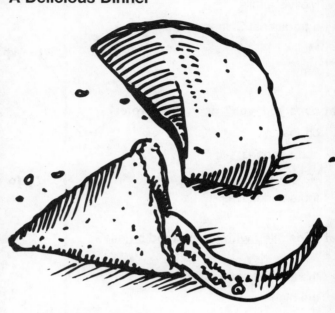

Molly is Chinese-American. Her family members gather together and serve a traditional Chinese meal once a week. Molly invited her friend Amy to join them for <u>it</u> this week.

Molly's family was busy preparing for dinner when Amy arrived. Molly directed Amy through the living room to the kitchen, which was <u>filled with many good smells.</u> "You can help me set the table," Molly told her friend. They laid the place settings on the table. They gave each person a pair of chopsticks, a soup bowl, a soup spoon, and a rice bowl on a saucer.

"Where are the forks and knives?" Amy asked.

"Oh, <u>you won't need those,</u>" Molly explained. "We use chopsticks. Don't worry, I'll show you how to use them."

The two girls went into the kitchen. Molly's father was slicing and chopping vegetables. He threw the vegetables into a large cooking pan coated with hot oil. "That's a *wok,*" Molly said. Amy watched the vegetables sizzle.

Molly's mother scooped different foods onto big plates. She asked the girls to carry the food-filled plates out to the table. Amy carried steamed rice. <u>It was one of the few dishes</u> she recognized. There were <u>meat-filled bundles</u> called *wontons,* steamed noodles, stir-fried beef, sweet-and-sour chicken, and pork spareribs. The food was nutritious and seasoned with herbs, spices, and sauces.

Once everyone was at the table, they quickly began eating. Their chopsticks moved quickly and made small clicking noises as they grabbed the food.

Amy was a little nervous about eating with chopsticks. Molly gave her instructions on how to hold and pinch with the chopsticks.

Amy finally managed to pick up a piece of chicken in her chopsticks. Suddenly, her fingers slipped, and the chicken flew across the table. <u>It landed in Molly's soup</u> with a splash. Everyone smiled. Molly's grandmother, who came every week to the family meal, patted Amy on the arm.

"We keep these on hand for emergencies," Molly's father said kindly. He brought out a fork and knife. He handed them to Amy.

Amy was relieved. She ate the rest of her dinner easily. It was delicious!

At the end of the meal, Amy was given a fortune cookie. <u>Amy broke hers open</u> and read it. "If you practice hard, you will learn many things." Amy laughed and said, "If you let me take home a pair of chopsticks, my fortune may come true!"

GO

DIRECTIONS: Look back at the words that are underlined in the story. Then answer the following questions.

1. **To what does <u>it</u> refer in the first paragraph?**
   - (A) Molly's family
   - (B) a traditional Chinese meal
   - (C) Molly
   - (D) Amy

2. **To what does <u>you won't need those</u> refer?**
   - (F) chopsticks
   - (G) soup spoons
   - (H) soup bowls
   - (J) forks and knives

3. **To what does <u>filled with many good smells</u> refer?**
   - (A) the living room
   - (B) the dinner
   - (C) the kitchen
   - (D) the house

4. **What <u>was one of the few dishes</u> Amy recognized?**
   - (F) stir-fried beef
   - (G) steamed noodles
   - (H) steamed rice
   - (J) sweet-and-sour chicken

5. **<u>Meat-filled bundles</u> refers to which kind of food?**
   - (A) wontons
   - (B) spareribs
   - (C) steamed noodles
   - (D) sweet-and-sour chicken

6. **What <u>landed in Molly's soup</u>?**
   - (F) wontons
   - (G) soup spoon
   - (H) chopsticks
   - (J) chicken

7. **To what does <u>Amy broke hers open</u> refer?**
   - (A) paper
   - (B) fortune
   - (C) chopsticks
   - (D) fortune cookie

STOP

Name _____ Date _____

Read with
Understanding
and Fluency

Using Prior Knowledge to Make Judgments

DIRECTIONS: Before reading the passage below, examine the following information:

- Ancient Greece existed over 2,000 years ago.
- The ancient Greeks developed democracy, a way of life that allowed the people to take part in their own government.
- The people of ancient Greece worshipped many different gods. Each year they celebrated festivals in honor of their gods. The most famous festival was called the Olympic Games.
- The people of ancient Greece ate only two meals a day.
- The men and women of ancient Greece wore cloaks and sandals.

Now read the passage and answer the questions based on your knowledge of ancient Greece.

> Ancient Rome was a powerful civilization that began almost 3,000 years ago. The ancient Romans were very interested in law and government. One principle they established that is still in use today is called *equity*. It means that a law should be flexible enough to fit different circumstances.
>
> Dinner was the largest of the three meals eaten each day, often served as a banquet. Clothing was simple and comfortable, and both men and women wore a short-sleeved garment called a *tunica*. Men wore a draped cloth, called a *toga*, over the tunica.
>
> The Romans worshiped many gods. The Romans later adopted some of the Greek gods and goddesses and gave them new names. For example, the Greek goddess Aphrodite became the Roman goddess Venus.
>
> The ancient Romans were famous for their many festivals, which were usually held in the huge open theater called the *Colosseum*. The Colosseum is still standing today. One of the most popular events was the chariot race, which was held in a large arena called a *circus*. The largest circus in ancient Rome was the Circus Maximus, which held 180,000 Roman spectators.

1. **Which society existed first—ancient Greece or ancient Rome?** _____

2. **True or false: Romans developed the concept of democracy.** _____

3. **True or false: The Olympic Games originated in ancient Rome.** _____

4. **Based on the reading, which of the following is an accurate judgment?**

   (A) The people in both societies were concerned about how they dressed.

   (B) Neither society cared much about festivals.

   (C) Worshipping many different gods was important to the people in both societies.

   (D) The people in both societies liked to eat a lot.

Name _____ Date _____

Reading

1B.5

Read with
**Understanding
and Fluency**

Finding Significant/ Minor Details

A Brave Young Woman

(1) Imagine a 17-year-old girl going to her king and telling him she would like to lead his army to victory. Even more amazing, imagine the king agreeing with her. You may think this is a far-fetched story, but it really happened.

(2) The year was 1429. Joan of Arc was only 17 years old when she went to King Charles VII of France to tell him she had seen a vision and heard the voices of saints. God wanted her to free France from the English. She was to lead the French army in battle against the English at Orleans.

(3) The king wanted to test her to see if she really did possess extraordinary powers. He disguised himself and put one of his noblemen on the throne. Joan saw right through the disguise and went immediately to the real king with her request. He tested her again, and she was able to tell him what he prayed to God when he was alone. The king was convinced of her powers.

(4) Joan and her army went to Orleans in April of 1429 and defeated the English in only ten days. Charles had never been officially crowned king because the city of Reims, the coronation site for French kings, was in enemy territory. After the victory at Orleans, Joan escorted Charles to Reims, where he was crowned King on July 17, 1429.

(5) Joan wanted to free France completely from the English, so she went again into battle outside Paris. This time she was wounded and captured by the English. Rather than return her to the French in exchange for a ransom, as was the custom, the English kept her as a prisoner.

(6) Like the French, the English also believed Joan had supernatural powers. Where the French king thought they came from God, the English thought they were from the devil. Joan was charged with witchcraft by a French tribunal sympathetic to the English. She was found guilty and burned at the stake on May 30, 1431, in Rouen, France. Her ashes were thrown into the Seine River.

(7) Later, her family requested a new trial, and in 1456, she was found innocent. Although it was too late to save her life, she was declared a saint. Saint Joan of Arc is recognized on the date of her death, May 30.

DIRECTIONS: Circle the answer that best tells the most significant detail of each numbered paragraph.

1.
   (A) Something amazing might happen involving a 17-year-old girl and a king.
   (B) This story is not possible; therefore, it is fiction.
   (C) A story about a girl asking her king if she may lead his army is really true.
   (D) A 17-year-old girl believed she could lead an army.

2.
   (F) Joan of Arc led the French army in a battle at Orleans.
   (G) Joan was 17 when she went to see the king.
   (H) Joan heard voices telling her to lead the French in battle.
   (J) This story took place in 1429.

3.
   (A) Joan was a good test-taker.
   (B) The king put a noble man on his throne.
   (C) The king tested Joan to see if what she claimed was true.
   (D) She did not pass the first test, so she had to take another.

4.
   (F) Joan was a military genius who defeated the English.
   (G) The king was not officially crowned because the English held Reims.
   (H) Joan led her army to victory in ten days.
   (J) After defeating the English, Joan led the king to Reims to be officially crowned.

5.
   (A) Joan liked wars, so she kept fighting until her capture by the English.
   (B) In a battle near Paris, Joan was wounded, captured, and held prisoner by the English.
   (C) The French army would not pay a ransom to the English to get Joan back.
   (D) Joan went into another battle outside Paris.

6.
   (F) Both the English and French thought Joan had supernatural powers.
   (G) Joan was tried for witchcraft and burned at the stake.
   (H) There is a debate about whether Joan's power came from God or the devil.
   (J) Joan's ashes were thrown into the Seine River.

7.
   (A) Joan's family wanted to bring her back to life, so they requested a new trial.
   (B) The new trial took place in 1456.
   (C) Joan was later found innocent and declared to be a saint.
   (D) Joan is recognized on the date of her death.

STOP

Clarifying Meaning

The Panama Canal

When the Panama Canal was completed in 1914, it became one of the greatest engineering wonders in the world. Built by the United States, the canal is a waterway that cuts across the Isthmus of Panama. It links the Atlantic Ocean and the Pacific Ocean. Prior to the opening of the Panama Canal, ships traveling from one ocean to the other had to sail around South America. With the canal, ships sailed approximately 6,000 miles traveling from New York to San Francisco. Before the canal opened, ships sailed more than 15,000 miles to make the same voyage.

For hundreds of years, people knew the importance of a waterway across Central America. In 1903, the United States signed a treaty with Panama, which allowed the United States to build and operate a canal.

One of the first obstacles to overcome in building the canal was disease, which plagued the Isthmus of Panama. Special medical teams went to the area to improve sanitary conditions. Efforts were made to rid the area of mosquitoes, which carried malaria and yellow fever.

In 1906, it was decided that the canal would be built as a series of locks. The locks would be cheaper and quicker to build. In 1907, an army engineer named Colonel George Goethals was put in charge of the project. Construction began with three main tasks: excavate earth to clear passages, build a dam across the Chagres River, and build the series of locks. Thousands of workers used steam shovels and dredges to cut passages through hills, swamps, and jungles.

The completed canal cost $380 million. It runs 50 miles across the Isthmus of Panama from Limon Bay in the Atlantic to the Bay of Panama in the Pacific. The water in the canal is controlled by three sets of locks, or water-filled chambers. Each lock is 110 feet wide and 70 feet deep. All but the very largest of today's ships can pass through the canal.

In 1977, the Panama Canal Treaty was signed. In this treaty, the United States transferred the responsibility for administration, upkeep, and maintenance of the canal to the Republic of Panama. On December 31, 1999, the transfer of authority was completed.

Name _____ Date _____

DIRECTIONS: Fill in the correct answers to complete the summary paragraph below.

The Panama Canal was completed in

(1) _____ .

It became one of the greatest engineering wonders in

the world. The canal was built by

(2) _____

and cuts across the

(3) _____ of **(4)** _____ .

The Panama Canal links the

(5) _____ Ocean

and the **(6)** _____ Ocean.

DIRECTIONS: Complete the statements below.

7. **The main reason for building the canal was**

_____

_____

_____

8. **One of the first major obstacles to overcome in building the canal was**

_____

_____

Construction of the canal began with three major tasks:

9. _____

10. _____

11. _____

Three facts about the completed canal:

12. _____

13. _____

14. _____

Summarize the role of each country with the canal in the past and in the present.

15. **The Republic of Panama**

_____

_____

_____

_____

16. **The United States**

_____

_____

_____

_____

_____

Summarize the two major treaties between the United States and the Republic of Panama.

17. 1903 _____

_____

_____

18. 1977 _____

_____

_____

STOP

Identifying Structure to Improve Comprehension

Television

The invention of the television changed the world in many important ways. Television has given people the opportunity to see and hear people, places, and events from around the world. Over 98 percent of all U.S. homes have a television. Television is now an important form of communication, allowing people instant access to current events.

Television does not have just one inventor. In the 1800s, an Italian inventor named Marconi discovered how to send signals through the air as electromagnetic waves. His invention was the radio. This set the stage for the invention of television. In the early 1900s, a young American named Philo Farnsworth began experimenting. He had an idea to send pictures as well as sound through the air. This idea resulted in the invention of the electronic television camera.

About the same time, an American scientist named Vladimir Zworykin invented the iconoscope and the kinescope. The iconoscope was a television camera. The kinescope was a picture tube to receive and show the picture. In 1929, Zworykin made the first television system.

But how does a television work? The picture that you see is the result of three steps. First, light and sound waves are changed into electronic signals. The light and sound waves come from the scene that is being televised. Next, these electronic signals are passed through the air to be received by individual television sets. Last, the television set unscrambles the signals. In this way, a picture is "moved" from the original scene to your television set.

These three steps happen because light and sound waves can be made into electronic signals. Light waves are picked up and changed into electronic signals by a camera. Sound waves are picked up and changed into electronic signals by a microphone. The camera signals are called *video,* and the microphone signals are called *audio.*

To produce electric signals in color, certain color signals are added to the video. Three primary colors of light—red, blue, and green—are used to produce pictures in color.

With the advent of digital technology, televisions have wider screens and pictures that are even clearer.

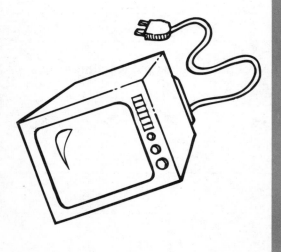

GO

DIRECTIONS: Fill in the chart below with information from the passage.

Cause	Effect
1.	Television pictures appear in color.
A camera picks up light waves.	2.
Vladimir Zworykin invents the iconoscope and the kinescope.	3.
4.	The electronic television camera is invented.
5.	People can see and hear people, places, and events from around the world.
Over 98 percent of all U.S. homes have a television.	6.
7.	Electronic signals are received by television sets.
Marconi invents the radio.	8.
9.	A picture is "moved" from the original scene to a television set.
Digital technology is becoming readily available.	10.

STOP

Name _____   Date _____

Reading
1B.8

Read with
Understanding
and Fluency

Organizing Information

The Hot-Air Balloon

For thousands of years, people have been fascinated with the idea of flying. The idea was especially appealing to two French brothers, Jacques and Joseph Montgolfier. In the late 1700s, they began experimenting with the idea of a hot-air balloon.

Their first experiment was to fill small paper bags with smoke. They found that the bags would rise in the air. The Montgolfiers first believed that the smoke made the bags rise. But later, they realized it was the hot air, not the smoke itself, that caused the bags to rise.

The Montgolfier brothers continued to experiment. In 1783, they put a hot-air balloon in the air for eight minutes. The balloon carried a rooster, a sheep, and a duck! They landed safely after history's first real balloon flight.

Later that year, French scientist Jean de Rozier and French nobleman Marquis d'Arlandes became the first people to make a free flight in a hot-air balloon. The balloon was made by the Montgolfier brothers. It rose over 300 feet into the air. The flight lasted 25 minutes as de Rozier floated over Paris, France.

About the same time that the Montgolfier brothers were making their hot-air balloons, another Frenchman, named Jacques Charles, was making a balloon that was filled with hydrogen, a gas that is lighter than air. In December of 1783, Charles made the first flight in a hydrogen balloon. His balloon rose over 2,000 feet into the air. He flew 25 miles from where he started.

In 1784, ballooning became very popular in France. People traveled for miles to see balloons take off and land. Many of the balloonists became heroes. On January 7, 1785, two men made the first balloon flight across the English Channel. The flight from England to France took two hours.

Through the years, balloons have been used for sport. But since their invention, balloons have been used for more serious purposes, too. In the 1700s and 1800s, balloons were used in wars to observe the enemy troops. In 1863, an American balloonist named Thaddeus Lowe directed a balloon corps that flew for the Union Army. Balloons were also used in World War I and World War II.

Today, hot-air balloons are made of nylon or polyester. To fly a balloon, the pilot burns fuel to produce hot air, which inflates the balloon. The balloon rises into the air as more hot air is produced. To lower the balloon, hot air is released.

Name _____ Date _____

DIRECTIONS: Fill in the timeline below with five important events in the history of hot-air ballooning from 1783 to 1863.

1.

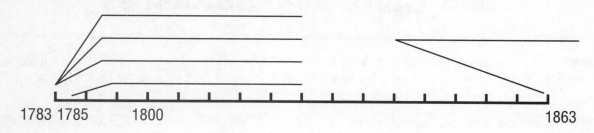

1783 1785   1800   1863

DIRECTIONS: Answer the following questions based on the passage.

2. **The main purpose of the article is _____ .**
   - (A) to examine the contributions of the Montgolfier brothers
   - (B) to explore the differences between hot-air balloons and hydrogen balloons
   - (C) to review the early history of hot-air ballooning in France
   - (D) to compare hot-air balloons of the past and present

3. **Through the years, balloons have been used _____ .**
   - (F) to carry animals
   - (G) to observe enemy troops
   - (H) for sport
   - (J) all of the above

4. **Which of the following puts the hot-air balloon creations of the Montgolfier brothers in the correct order?**
   - (A) smoke-filled bags, hot-air balloon carrying animals, hot-air balloon carrying a person
   - (B) hot-air balloon carrying animals, hot air balloon carrying a person, hydrogen balloon
   - (C) smoke-filled bags, hot-air balloon carrying a person, hydrogen balloon
   - (D) hydrogen balloon, smoke-filled bags, hot-air balloon carrying people

DIRECTIONS: Write a *T* if the statement is true and an *F* if the statement is false.

5. _____ **In 1783, the Montgolfier brothers put a hot-air balloon in the air.**

6. _____ **Smoke made hot-air balloons rise.**

7. _____ **One of the first balloons carried a dog, mule, and duck.**

8. _____ **Jean de Rozier was one of the first people to ride in a hot-air balloon.**

9. _____ **His flight lasted 25 minutes as he floated over Paris.**

10. _____ **The Montgolfiers' balloons were filled with hydrogen.**

STOP

Reading

1B.9

Self-Monitoring and
Self-Correcting Strategies

DIRECTIONS: Skim the passage first, then read the questions. Then read the passage more closely, thinking about the questions as you read. Choose the answer for each question that follows the passage.

Floating the River

"Aren't we there yet?" Shiloh asked. At last, she and her family were on their way to their annual tubing trip. Floating down Glenn River on an inner tube was one of Shiloh's favorite things. This year they would float five whole miles, all the way to Glenn Fork.

With each passing mile, Shiloh smiled more and more as she thought of the fun they would have. When they finally reached Glenn Fork and parked the car, she jumped out, all ready to go.

"Not so fast, Shiloh," said her mother. "Remember, we're just here to leave the car. We still have to drive up the river. After we float back here, we'll be able to drive the car upstream to the truck. Otherwise, we won't have any way to get home."

"Oh, yeah, false alarm," Shiloh said. She had forgotten the family's plan to leave one car at each end of the float.

The whole family piled into the truck and drove to Jenkins Bar. Shiloh's father helped her unload her backpack and shiny tube from the truck. They walked down to the river's bank and put their toes in the water. Shiloh gasped as she felt how cold the water was. She took a deep breath and pushed herself out into the river. As Shiloh followed her family downstream, she thought to herself, "This will be the best tubing trip ever!"

1. This story is mostly about _____ .

  (A) driving a truck

  (B) a family's adventure

  (C) a family's argument

  (D) a family's business

2. The family will float between which two points?

  (F) from Jenkins Bar to Glenn Fork

  (G) from Glenn Fork to Glenn River

  (H) from Glenn River to Jenkins Bar

  (J) from Glenn Fork to Jenkins Bar

3. How do you think Shiloh's parents feel about the tubing trip?

  (A) bored

  (B) disappointed

  (C) frustrated

  (D) excited

4. Why is the family driving both a car and a truck?

  (F) so they don't get the truck wet and muddy

  (G) so they can show that they have a lot of money

  (H) so they can all have a ride to the river

  (J) so they can have transportation back to where they started

5. Which character do you learn the most about in this passage?

  (A) Shiloh's mother

  (B) Shiloh

  (C) Shiloh's father

  (D) Shiloh's sister

Reading

1B

For pages 19–32

Mini-Test 2

DIRECTIONS: Read the story and answer the questions that follow.

Mammal, Fish, or Fowl?

When scientists in England received reports from Australia about the duckbill platypus in the late 1700s, they thought they were the victims of a hoax. Surely, they must have reasoned, some jokester had sewn body parts from several different animals together in an attempt to trick them. Indeed, the duckbill platypus is a strange animal. It has a bill resembling a duck, a flat, paddleshaped tail like a beaver, and it scuffles along the ground in the manner of an alligator. Both its front and hind feet are webbed and have claws. Unlike most mammals, it has neither lips nor exterior ears. Although it nurses its young, it does not give birth to live babies. Instead it lays eggs—like a chicken! Small wonder that scientists were confused and not certain whether they were dealing with fish, fowl, or some kind of new species. They eventually classified the platypus with mammals.

1. **This story mostly describes _____ .**

   (A) why scientists decided that the platypus was a mammal

   (B) the unique features of the platypus

   (C) where the platypus can be found

   (D) a scientific hoax

2. **Which sentence is probably true?**

   (F) One scientist probably made the decision on how the platypus would be classified.

   (G) Scientists were probably in complete agreement on how to classify the platypus.

   (H) Scientists probably debated over how the platypus should be classified.

   (J) Scientists probably let the people of England vote on how the platypus should be classified.

3. **Which of the following statements is false?**

   (A) The platypus has a tail that resembles a beaver's tail.

   (B) English scientists first learned about the platypus in the late 1700s.

   (C) The platypus does not have lips.

   (D) The platypus is a type of bird.

4. **Which of these characteristics would have helped the scientists decide that the platypus was a mammal?**

   (F) The platypus nurses its young.

   (G) The platypus lays eggs.

   (H) The platypus does not have external ears.

   (J) The platypus has a bill like a duck.

STOP

Reading Standards

Read with Understanding and Fluency

Goal 1: Read with understanding and fluency.

Learning Standard 1A *(See page 7.)*

Learning Standard 1B *(See page 18.)*

Learning Standard 1C—Students who meet the standard can comprehend a broad range of reading materials.

1. Use evidence in text to form and refine questions, predictions, and hypotheses. *(See page 35.)*
2. Ask open-ended questions. *(See page 36.)*
3. Identify evidence for inferences and interpretations based on text combined with prior knowledge. *(See pages 37–38.)*
4. Compare the content and organization (e.g., themes, topics, text structure, story elements) of various selections. *(See pages 39–40.)*
5. Recognize similarities/differences of varying styles or points of view. *(See page 41.)*
6. Select reading strategies for text appropriate to the reader's purpose. *(See page 42.)*
7. Synthesize key points (ideas) and supporting details to form conclusions. *(See pages 43–44.)*
8. Interpret imagery and figurative language (e.g., alliteration, metaphor, simile, personification). *(See pages 45–46.)*
9. Explain how authors and illustrators use text and art to express their ideas (e.g., points of view, design hues, metaphors). *(See page 47.)*
10. Show examples of cultural styles in art to enhance meaning and comprehension as done by different illustrators.
11. Interpret information from tables, maps, visual aids, and charts to enhance understanding of text. *(See page 48.)*
12. Apply appropriate reading strategies to fiction and nonfiction texts within and across content areas. *(See page 49.)*

Reading

1C.1

Making and Refining Predictions

DIRECTIONS: Before you read the passage about cross-country and downhill skiing below, make the following predictions. Then after you read the passage, refine your answers as needed based on what you have read.

1. **Which type of skiing is easiest to do—cross-country or downhill? Why do you think so?**

_____

_____

_____

_____

2. **Which type of skiing is the most expensive to do? Explain your answer.**

_____

_____

_____

_____

Cross-Country or Downhill?

The answer to this question makes a big difference if you are a skier. Both forms of skiing are popular and can be done by people of all ages. Both require snow, and both can be done for relaxation or competition. So what is it that makes the two methods of skiing so different?

Cross-country skiing means just that—you ski across the country. You do not need tall hills or ski lifts to ski cross-country. You simply need snow and equipment. Cross-country skiers can go skiing right outside their back door. Even land that is completely flat can be enjoyable for the cross-country skier. Cross-country races can be 50 minutes long or two hours long. These long races require strength and endurance. Races vary in length from 9 miles to 30 miles.

Downhill skiing is also named for the activity. A downhill skier skis down hills. That means the skier needs tall hills and a way to get up to the top. Downhill skiing takes place at ski resorts. Downhill races are short. The goal is to get down the hill the fastest without falling. Speed is the goal, and downhill racers can go faster than 80 miles per hour.

Both types of skiing require special equipment. Downhill skis are wider and shorter than cross-country skis. The boots are also different. Downhill boots are larger and protect the ankles from injury. They are connected to the ski at the heel and toe with a binding. Cross-country boots are flexible, like shoes, and usually fit below the ankle. They are attached to the ski at the toe only. Both types of skiing require ski poles. A downhill skier uses poles for balance and direction, whereas a cross-country skier uses poles as part of the glide-step technique.

Both forms of skiing are great exercise, but cross-country skiing has the potential to burn more calories. Cross-country skiing at a pace of 5 to 8 miles an hour can burn 9 to 13 calories per minute. Downhill skiing at a moderate pace burns 6 calories per minute. No matter which form of skiing you choose, you will be doing something good for your body.

Asking Open-Ended Questions

DIRECTIONS: As you read the following passage, write down three open-ended questions that will help you determine the author's purpose and meaning. (An example question is provided.) Then answer the questions you wrote.

Clue "Close-ended" questions can be answered with yes/no or similar simple responses. "Open-ended" questions allow more varied and elaborate answers than close-ended questions. Asking open-ended questions as you read can help you better understand the material.

The World Series

Baseball is an important part of American culture and history. The World Series is the most exciting and important sporting event of the year because it names the national champion in America's favorite pastime.

In spite of what the title says, the World Series is actually not a championship open to the world. The World Series matches the American League champion team against the National League champion team. The first team to win four games out of seven wins the World Series.

The World Series was first played in 1903. The American League champions, the Boston Pilgrims, played the National League champions, the Pittsburgh Pirates. The Boston Pilgrims, now named the Boston Red Sox, won this first World Series.

Although the World Series seemed to be off to a great start in 1903, the next year was a different story. In 1904, the New York Giants refused to play the Boston Pilgrims in the World Series. To this day, no one is sure why they refused, but 1904 was the only year in World Series history that did not have a world championship series.

For a team to make it to the World Series takes months of hard work and a lot of talent. Most teams play more than 160 games between April and October of each year. Many great baseball players, such as Babe Ruth, Jackie Robinson, Joe DiMaggio, and Lou Gehrig, have played in the World Series.

Many World Series records have been broken over the years. But in 1956, a little-known player named Don Larsen pitched a no-hitter game for the New York Yankees. His record has never been broken.

The New York Yankees have won more World Series championships than any team in history. No matter who wins the title, the World Series remains one of the most popular events each year for sports fans. In fact, there is even a World Series for the youngest players. Unlike the adult World Series, the Little League World Series includes teams from other countries. Taiwan has won more of the series than any other country.

1. **What is the author's purpose in writing this passage?**

2. _____

3. _____

4. _____

STOP

Making Inferences

DIRECTIONS: Read the passage and answer the questions on the next page.

Save the Elephants

Elephants are peaceful and magnificent animals. They live in social groups similar to families with one female elephant, called a *matriarch,* leading the herd. As one of the largest land mammals in the world, African elephants have few predators. In fact, one of the greatest dangers to elephants in past years has not been from another animal but from humans. The value of the ivory tusks on the elephants was irresistible to greedy hunters.

African elephants that live on the grassy savanna have long, curved tusks. Some African elephants live in forest areas. They have shorter tusks, allowing them to move more freely through the crowded forest. Both male and female elephants have tusks, which they use as a tool. Elephants tend to prefer either a right or left tusk, just as we favor our right or left hand. The tusk they use most often becomes shorter.

During the 1980s, the African elephant population was a casualty of human desires. The number of elephants declined from well over 1 million to about 600,000. It is estimated that more than 270 elephants were killed each day! Thousands of baby elephants, called *calves,* were left to take care of themselves. The African elephant was in a dangerous situation.

What was happening to the elephants? They were being killed by poachers who wanted their ivory tusks. In many poor countries, poaching was one of the few ways to earn money. The ivory was valued around the world. It has been used for jewelry, statues, knife handles, billiard balls, piano keys, and other products.

Organizations that protect animals and look out for their welfare were outraged. They devised a plan to alleviate the situation. They began a publicity campaign to spread awareness of the problem. Some large companies helped by refusing to buy ivory and asking their customers to do the same.

International laws were eventually passed to help make the killing of elephants less appealing. The sale of ivory was made illegal all around the world.

In recent days, "paintings" made by elephants have been used to raise money for elephant protection. Elephants use their trunks to hold the paintbrush. The paintings are then sold with the money going toward conservation efforts.

DIRECTIONS: Answer the following questions.

1. **What could you learn about elephants by looking at their tusks?**

   _____

   _____

   _____

   _____

   _____

2. **What do you think would have happened to the African elephant if no one had made any changes?**

   _____

   _____

   _____

   _____

   _____

3. **What is a poacher?**

   _____

   _____

   _____

   _____

4. **How do you think poachers were affected when ivory trade became illegal?**

   _____

   _____

   _____

   _____

5. **What might happen to elephants if ivory trade was made legal again?**

   _____

   _____

   _____

   _____

6. **What is the best way to continue to protect the elephants?**

   _____

   _____

   _____

   _____

STOP

Name _____ Date _____

Reading
1C.4

Read with
Understanding
and Fluency

Comparing Various Selections

Pen Pals

Dear Yena,

My name is Li Lui. I am 10 years old. I live in Beijing, China. My parents and I live in a tall apartment building. Our city has more than 10 million people. It is a busy city with crowded sidewalks and lots to do.

I like school. I attend from 7:00 A.M. until 4:30 P.M. My favorite subjects are art and Chinese. I don't like math at all, but I have to study it every day! I wear a blue school uniform that looks like a warm-up suit.

I love drawing, watching TV, and eating. My favorite shows are cartoons. My favorite food is shrimp chips. We eat a lot of rice, fish, and vegetables. We eat fish for breakfast to start the day with protein for strength. I like to drink soda.

When I grow up, I'd like to be a fashion designer. I want to design beautiful clothes for famous people to wear. Then, when I go to the movies, I can say, "I created that outfit!"

I'm glad to have a pen pal from another country. I hope you are having a nice day! Please write soon.

Sincerely,
Li Lui

Dear Li Lui,

Thank you for writing! I am excited to have a pen pal from China. Your country seems exotic to me. I live in Accra, the capital of Ghana. My home is a one-floor house on a quiet street. I live with my parents and grandmother.

I enjoy school most of the time. My favorite subject is science. I want to be a pediatrician when I grow up so I can help heal sick children. I'm not so good at French. I need to practice more, but I find it so dull! I wear a uniform to school, too. It's a brown dress with a yellow shirt.

My favorite television programs are cartoons, too. Maybe we watch the same shows. I love to eat plantains. They're similar to bananas. I could eat them all day! I eat a lot of rice, also. I like fruit juice better than soda, though.

We have lots in common! I hope you are doing well, and I look forward to your reply.

Sincerely,
Yena

GO

Name _____ Date _____

DIRECTIONS: Fill in the webs with information from the pen-pal letters. Write Li Lui's information on the left and Yena's information on the right. Draw stars next to the answers they have in common.

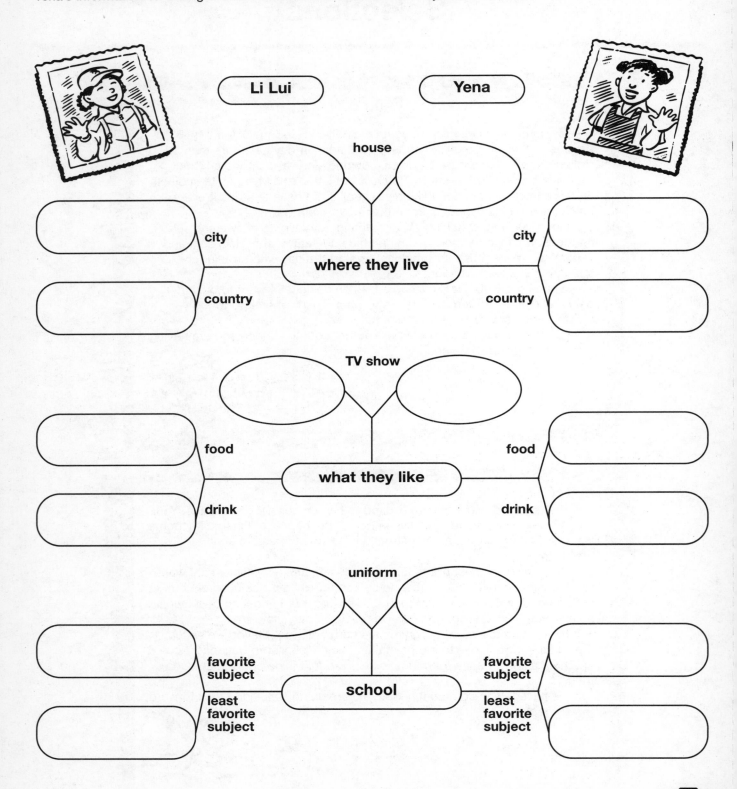

Li Lui

Yena

house

city

country

where they live

city

country

TV show

food

drink

what they like

food

drink

uniform

favorite subject

least favorite subject

school

favorite subject

least favorite subject

STOP

Reading

1C.5

Comparing Different Styles and Points of View

DIRECTIONS: Read the selections that follow, then answer the questions.

February 10

I did it! Well, I didn't win first place, but I came in second. And I'm really proud of that.

At first, I was scared when I looked out and saw all those people in the audience. I was afraid I'd forget everything. But then I told myself, "You studied hard. You know all those words. Come on, you can do it!"

My first word was *indicate:* i-n-d-i-c-a-t-e. It was easy. Then I knew I could do the rest of them, too. The only word that really stumped me was *cannibal.* I spelled it c-a-n-n-i-b-l-e—oops. Rebecca spelled it right, along with her last word: *hydraulics.*

Oh well. I won a dictionary and had my picture taken for the newspaper. When I came home, my family had a party to celebrate! Tomorrow, I start studying for next year's contest.

Local Boy Finishes Second in Regional Spelling Bee

February 10—Ben Hanson, age 10, of Park Creek, finished second in the Regional Spelling Bee sponsored by the Literacy Society. He spelled eight words correctly, finally stumbling over the word *cannibal.* Hanson won a new dictionary for his efforts.

Rebecca Cohen, from Detroit, Michigan, won first prize for spelling the word *hydraulics.* She will receive a $100 savings bond and go on to the National Spelling Bee held in Washington, DC, next month.

1. **Who wrote the first passage? Where did the second passage appear?**

_____

_____

_____

2. **Name three similarities between the passages.**

_____

_____

_____

3. **Name three differences between the passages.**

_____

_____

_____

STOP

Matching Reading Strategies to Your Purpose

DIRECTIONS: Wanda is writing a report about the future uses of computers, telephones, and televisions. Keep this purpose in mind when you answer the questions.

1. **In doing her report, Wanda used the book titled *Technology Tomorrow*. Where in the book should Wanda look to learn what information is found in each chapter?**

   Ⓐ the index

   Ⓑ the table of contents

   Ⓒ the title page

   Ⓓ the introduction

2. **Which of these would Wanda *not* want to include in her report?**

   Ⓕ ways that people will use television to improve their education

   Ⓖ how telephones will allow more people to work at home

   Ⓗ the ways in which computers and televisions can be connected

   Ⓙ a description of the newest kitchen appliances

DIRECTIONS: For number 3, read the sentence. Then choose the key words Wanda should include in her notes about technology.

3. **In the coming years, telephones, televisions, and computers will become much more powerful, and they will serve many of the same purposes.**

   Ⓐ telephones, televisions, and computers made by some companies

   Ⓑ same methods used to make telephones, televisions, and computers

   Ⓒ telephones, televisions, and computers to be more powerful and more similar

   Ⓓ more powerful computers will replace televisions and computers

DIRECTIONS: Choose the best answer.

Index

Engines

fuel, 32–36

types of, 30–38

History

in Africa, 18–22

in Asia, 20–24

in Europe, 2–10

in North America, 8–18

in South America, 16–18

legends and stories, 72–78

Tracks

laying, 26–32

types, 28–33, 93–95

Workers

job classifications, 80–85

unions, 4–8

---

4. **The index above appears in a book about trains. Which pages would probably tell about a Ghost Train some people say they have seen?**

   Ⓕ 72–78

   Ⓖ 32–36

   Ⓗ 80–85

   Ⓙ 28–33

5. **Which pages would give you information on trains that ran between France and Germany during the 1930s?**

   Ⓐ 4–8

   Ⓑ 18–22

   Ⓒ 2–10

   Ⓓ 16–18

Synthesizing Key Points

The Great Wall of China

The Great Wall of China is the longest structure ever built. Constructed entirely by hand, the Great Wall winds 4,000 miles along the mountains across northern China. This massive wall is even visible from space.

During 400 B.C., small stretches of the wall were built to protect the country from invaders. During the Ch'in Dynasty from 221–206 B.C., these first walls were connected together in a new and much longer wall. Work on the wall continued through the Han, Sui, and Ming dynasties. It has been estimated that almost a million laborers worked on the Great Wall over a period of many years.

The main part of the Great Wall stretches 2,150 miles long. Special sections of loops and sidewalls add 1,800 more miles to the length of the wall. These sidewalls were added as an extra defense against invaders. The wall is approximately 25 feet high and 15 feet wide at the top. The core of the wall was made with heavily packed earth. The outer wall was finished with hand-cut stones. For every mile of wall built, over 422,400 cubic feet of material was needed.

To further reinforce the wall, watchtowers were built every 100 to 200 yards. The 40-foot high towers were stocked with food, water, and supplies for the defenders who were on guard at the wall.

Although the Great Wall was built to protect China from invaders, it was only successful with minor attacks. In the 1200s, a Mongol leader from the north named Genghis Khan led his army across the wall and conquered most of China.

Over the centuries, much of the Great Wall deteriorated. Today, three main sections of the wall have been rebuilt. One section is near the city of Peking. Another is in the province of Kansu in north-central China. The third restored section is along the country's east coast.

The Great Wall no longer exists for defense. Through the years, it has been incorporated into Chinese culture and myth. The most famous story tells of Meng Jiangnu, whose husband was killed in the construction of the wall. It is said that her tears caused a section of the wall to collapse.

GO

DIRECTIONS: Choose the correct answer.

1. **Choose the title that best reflects the main idea of this passage.**
   - (A) China's Wondrous Wall
   - (B) The Invaders of China
   - (C) China's Great Defense
   - (D) Watchtowers on the Wall

2. **Which of the following tells why the Great Wall of China was built?**
   - (F) to protect from invaders
   - (G) for quicker travel
   - (H) to honor the great dynasties
   - (J) to boost tourism

3. **Three sections of the wall have been rebuilt. They are _____ .**
   - (A) Han, Sui, and Ming
   - (B) near Peking, in the province of Kansu, and along the east coast
   - (C) in northern China, near Peking, and along the watchtowers
   - (D) Ming, in the province of Kansu, and near Peking

DIRECTIONS: Fill in the answer that correctly completes each sentence.

The Great Wall—

4. consists of a main section that is

   _____ miles long.

5. has special loops and sidewalls, which

   add _____ more miles to its length.

6. is approximately _____ feet high and

   _____ feet wide at the top.

7. has an outer wall made of hand-cut

   _____ .

Watchtowers—

8. were built every _____ to _____ yards.

9. are about _____ feet high.

10. are stocked with _____ ,

    _____ , and _____ .

DIRECTIONS: Write a few sentences explaining why you think the Great Wall was not successful in protecting China against invaders.

   _____

   _____

   _____

   _____

   _____

   _____

STOP

Reading

1C.8

Interpreting Imagery and Figurative Language

DIRECTIONS: Read the passage and answer the questions on the next page.

Sollie, the Rock

I've lived on a lake for most of my life. I've had lots of time to learn all sorts of fun things to do in the water. I think my favorite thing of all is water skiing. That's why I decided to invite my best friend, Sollie, over to give it a try.

Sollie had never been on skis before, but I knew Dad could help him learn, just like he helped me.

Water skiing is like flying. If you aren't afraid of getting up, you'll enjoy the ride. That's what I told Sollie before we spent the afternoon trying to get him up on skis for the first time.

I thought it would be easy. Sollie is a seal, sleek and smooth in the water, bobbing in and out of the waves. I thought someone so agile would find skiing easy. It didn't dawn on me until the fourth try that Sollie is shaped more like a rock than a bird.

On his first try, Sollie let go of the towrope when Dad hit the gas. He sank as fast as the *Titanic.* The only things visible were the tips of his skis.

On his second try, Sollie leaned into the skis, flipping head over heels like a gymnast falling off the balance beam. His skis formed an "X" that marked the spot where he disappeared.

On the third try, Sollie stood up. He teetered forward and then back, as if he were a rag doll. His biggest mistake was holding on to the rope after he lost both skis. He flopped about behind the boat like a giant carp until he finally let go.

On the fourth try, Sollie bent his knees, straightened his back, and flew around the lake behind the boat as if he were a professional skier. He jumped the wake, rolled out next to the boat, and waved at me. He was "the man."

After three times around the lake, Sollie let go of the rope. He returned to his former self and dropped into the water like a rock.

After spending the afternoon out on the water with me and Dad, Sollie fell in love with water skiing. We made plans to do it again soon. Maybe even a rock can learn to fly!

GO

Name _____ Date _____

DIRECTIONS: Answer the following questions about similes and metaphors in the story, *Sollie, the Rock*.

Metaphor—a direct comparison between unlike things. *Example:* Bobby is a mouse.

Simile—an indirect comparison between two unlike things using the words *like, as,* or *as if* to make the comparison. *Example:* Bobby is like a mouse.

Alliteration—the use of words that repeat the same beginning sound. *Example:* Round and round the rugged rock the ragged rascal ran.

1. **Identify the following lines as metaphors (M) or similes (S).**

   _____ Sollie is a seal, sleek and smooth in the water, bobbing in and out of the waves.

   _____ Sollie is shaped more like a rock than a bird.

   _____ He sank as fast as the *Titanic*.

   _____ He flopped about behind the boat like a giant carp until he finally let go.

2. **What do the above similes suggest about Sollie?**

   _____

   _____

   _____

   _____

   _____

   _____

3. **Why is the following sentence not a simile or a metaphor?**

   Sollie bent his knees, straightened his back, and flew around the lake behind the boat as if he were a professional skier.

   (A) It does not make a comparison.

   (B) It makes a comparison between like things.

   (C) It makes a contrast rather than a comparison.

   (D) The comparison is not between a person and an animal.

4. **Fill in the blank to turn the sentence into a simile.**

   Sollie bent his knees, straightened his back, and flew around the lake behind the boat . . .

   _____

   _____

   _____ .

5. **Identify the use of alliteration given in the fourth paragraph of the story.**

   _____

   _____

   _____

   _____

   _____

   _____

Reading

1C.9

Read with
Understanding
and Fluency

Understanding How Art Enhances Meaning

DIRECTIONS: Read the passage and answer the questions below.

Easter Island

Few places in the world are more intriguing and mystifying than Easter Island, located in the Pacific Ocean 2,300 miles from the coast of Chile. Easter Island has 64 square miles of rugged coastline and steep hills. Scientists believe the island began as a volcano. Three extinct volcanoes remain on the island. The largest one rises 1,400 feet high.

On Easter Sunday of 1722, Dutch Admiral Jacob Roggeveen and his crew landed on Easter Island aboard the Dutch ship *Arena.* The astonished crew found dozens of huge stone figures standing on long stone platforms. The statues, some measuring 40 feet tall, were similar in appearance. Their expressionless faces were without eyes. Huge red stone cylinders were placed on their heads. Since that time, the island has been a source of mystery and intrigue to scientists and explorers.

Scientists believe that the statues were carved from hard volcanic rock in the crater walls of the volcano called *Rana Raraku.* The statues were chiseled with stone picks made of basalt. Although the statues weigh many tons each, it is believed that they were moved with ropes and rollers across the island and placed on long platforms. This may be the reason for one island legend about the statues "walking" to their site.

Today, Easter Island is governed by Chile, a country of South America. Almost the entire population of 2,000 people live in the small village of Hanga Roa on the west coast of the island.

1. Summarize in two or three sentences the author's main purpose in writing this passage.

_____

_____

_____

2. Name two ways in which the author's purpose is enhanced by the accompanying art.

_____

_____

_____

Reading
1C.11

Interpreting Supplemental Information

DIRECTIONS: Use this timeline to answer the questions about the Internet.

The Beginning of the Internet

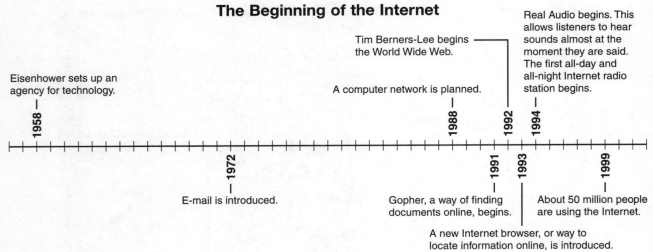

1. **When did Real Audio begin? Why was it important?**

   _____

   _____

   _____

2. **Did the World Wide Web begin before or after e-mail began?**

   _____

   _____

3. **Which event happened before 1960?**

   _____

   _____

   _____

4. **Which event happened during the 1980s?**

   _____

   _____

   _____

5. **How many events are included on the timeline?**

   _____

6. **By 1999, about how many people were using the Internet?**

   _____

STOP

Reading

Applying Appropriate Reading Strategies

Read with Understanding and Fluency

DIRECTIONS: Read the passages and answer the questions that follow.

A

Wasps build new nests every year. The potter wasp creates a mud "jar" nest for each of its eggs. The wasp then stings caterpillars to paralyze them and places them in the jar nests. The nests are sealed, and the caterpillars are used as food for the developing wasps.

B

Laura Ingalls Wilder wrote a series of nine children's books about her life as a pioneer. The first book was titled *Little House in the Big Woods.* Laura's books have been praised for their portrayals of life on the American frontier.

C

Ice hockey originated in the mid-1800s when British troops played games of field hockey on the frozen lakes and ponds of Canada's provinces of Ontario and Nova Scotia. It became Canada's national sport by the early 1900s. Since then, the sport has become popular in European countries such as Russia and Sweden, as well as in the United States.

D

One day, just as the leaves were beginning to change color, Rip Van Winkle walked through the woods and up the mountains. By early afternoon, he found himself on one of the highest points of the Catskill Mountains. By late afternoon, Rip was tired and panting, so he found a spot with a beautiful view where he could lay down and rest. Through an opening in the trees, Rip could see miles and miles of lower country and rich woodland. In the distance, he could view the mighty Hudson River. It was moving calmly along its course, showing reflections of the soft white clouds in the sky.

E

Chevy 1984 Cavalier. Has all 4 tires. Runs. May need work. You must haul it away yourself. $500 or best offer. Call Clutch at 555-4343.

F

As she walked along the sandy shore with delight at nature's wonders, she did see starfish, whitecaps, conch shells, and more. She knew that she would never fly free like the tissue-paper seagulls above or swim with the dolphins she did love.

1. **Which of the passages are non-fiction?**

   _____

2. **Which passage requires you to pay particular attention to figurative language?**

   _____

3. **Which passage would you be more likely to read with an eye to literal truth—passage B or passage D?**

   _____

4. **Which passage could you more easily illustrate on a timeline—passage C or passage E?**

   _____

5. **Which passage requires you to pay particular attention to a sequence of events—passage A or passage B?**

   _____

Mini-Test 3

DIRECTIONS: Read the story and answer the questions that follow.

The Eiffel Tower

The Eiffel Tower in Paris, France, is considered to be one of the Seven Wonders of the Modern World. The Eiffel Tower stands 984 feet high. It is made of a wrought-iron framework that rests on a base that is 330 square feet. The tower is made of 12,000 pieces of metal and two and a half million rivets. Elevators and stairways lead to the top of the tower.

Among other things, the Eiffel Tower contains restaurants and weather stations. Since 1953, it has been used as the main television transmitter for Paris. Before that, it was used to transmit radio signals and as a weather monitoring station.

Today, everyone agrees that the Eiffel Tower is a true wonder. But in 1887, many people believed that Alexander Gustave Eiffel was crazy when he began building his metal tower.

Gustave Eiffel designed his tower to be the centerpiece of the World's Fair exposition of 1889 in Paris. He was chosen for the project because he was, at age fifty-three, France's master builder. Eiffel was already famous for his work with iron, which included the framework for the Statue of Liberty.

On January 26, 1887, workers began digging the foundation for the Eiffel Tower. Everyone but Gustave Eiffel believed that it would be impossible to finish the tallest structure in the world in just two years. After all, it had taken 36 years to build the Washington Monument.

The French government would grant the project only one-fifth of the money needed. Eiffel himself agreed to provide $1,300,000, which he could recover if the tower was a financial success.

In March of 1889, after over two years of continuous work, the Eiffel Tower was completed. Eiffel not only met his deadline but also built the tower for less money than he thought it would cost. The final cost was exactly $1,505,675.90.

1. **What was Gustave Eiffel's opinion about whether the Eiffel Tower could be completed in two years? How did his opinion differ from other opinions around him?**

_____

_____

_____

_____

_____

2. **If you were an accountant simply looking at the money facts about the Eiffel Tower, would you judge it to be a success? Why or why not?**

_____

_____

_____

_____

_____

3. The first paragraph of the passage contains many facts about the Eiffel Tower. How do these facts help you understand the greatness of Gustave Eiffel's achievement?

_____

_____

_____

_____

_____

4. In your opinion, what is the best use of the Eiffel Tower—a shopping mall, a weather station, a communication transmitter, or a restaurant center? Why?

_____

_____

_____

_____

5. Using only facts from the story, prove that Gustave Eiffel was a success in life.

_____

_____

_____

_____

6. In your opinion, what makes a building famous?

_____

_____

_____

_____

STOP

Reading Standards

Read and Understand Literature

Goal 2: Read and understand literature representative of various societies, eras, and ideas.

Learning Standard 2A—Students who meet the standard can understand how literary elements and techniques are used to convey meaning.

1. Read a wide range of fiction.
2. Identify literary elements and techniques in literary genres (e.g., fables, biographies, historical fiction) and tell how they affect the story. *(See page 53.)*

What it means:

● The term *genre* often is used to refer to different forms of fiction, including novels, poetry, legends, myths, folktales, fables, biographies, and historical fiction.

3. Predict how the story might be different if the author changed literary elements or techniques (e.g., dialect, setting, vocabulary). *(See pages 54–55.)*
4. Explain how a technique or element affects the events or characterization in a literary work. *(See pages 56–57.)*
5. Make inferences about character traits and check text for verification. *(See pages 58–59.)*
6. Analyze the use of unfamiliar vocabulary. *(See page 60.)*
7. Use comprehension strategies (e.g., association, categorization, graphic organizers) to enhance understanding. *(See pages 61–62.)*
8. Identify ways in which fiction and nonfiction works are organized differently. *(See page 63.)*

Learning Standard 2B *(See page 65.)*

Name _____ Date _____

Identifying Literary Genres

DIRECTIONS: Read the passage and answer the questions that follow.

Fox and the Grapes

One warm summer day, a fox was walking along when he noticed a bunch of grapes on a vine above him. Cool, juicy grapes would taste so good. The more he thought about it, the more the fox wanted those grapes. He tried standing on his tiptoes. He tried jumping high in the air. He tried getting a running start before he jumped. But no matter what he tried, the fox could not reach the grapes. As he angrily walked away, the fox muttered, "They were probably sour anyway!"

Moral: A person (or fox) sometimes pretends that he does not want something that he or she cannot have.

1. **This passage is which genre (type) of literature?**

   Ⓐ poetry

   Ⓑ biography

   Ⓒ nonfiction

   Ⓓ fable

2. **What clues in the story helped you decide what genre it is?**

   _____

   _____

   _____

   _____

   _____

3. **Using the passage as an example, write a definition of this genre. Use the sentences below as a guide.**

   _____ is usually about

   _____

   _____

   _____ .

   _____ includes

   _____

   _____

   _____

   _____

   _____

   _____ .

STOP

Changing Elements in a Story

The Escape

Into the shady glen, the small figure rode on a pony that was little larger than a dog. The pony's breath misted in the crisp air as the beast blew air out of its nostrils. The green-mantled figure patted the neck of the beast, whispering words of comfort into the animal's ear. In response, the faithful steed nickered, thumped his wide hoofs twice upon the soft bed of the forest floor, and ceased its shaking.

"We've left the raiders behind, old friend," said Rowan, as she removed her hooded mantle and tossed her head back and forth, bringing peace to her own troubled mind. Rowan was one of four daughters of Sylvia, guide of all wood folk.

Suddenly, shouts of rough men cut through the glade's peace.

"In here, I tell ya. The maid's gone to hiding in this grove." "Nah, ya lunk. She'd never wait for us here. Not after she dunked old Stefan at the marsh. No! She's a gone on to her crazy folk, don'tcha know."

The two gray-cloaked riders dismounted, still arguing as they examined the earth for traces of the child's flight.

"Who was the lout who let her escape?" asked the first.

"'Tis one who no longer breathes the air so freely," returned the second grimly. "The lord nearly choked the fool, even as the knave begged for mercy. Ah, there's little patience for one who lets a mystic escape, to be true!"

Five nobly dressed horsemen wove through the trees to the clearing where these two rustics still squatted. In the lead came the fierce lord, a huge form with scarlet and gray finery worn over his coat of mail.

"What say you?" he roared. "Have you found the trail of Rowan?"

"No, sire," spoke the first gray, trembling, "though I was certain the child headed into this wood. Shall I continue to search, lord?"

"Aye, indeed," replied the master calmly, controlled. "She is here. I know it, too. You have a keen sense for the hunt, Mikkel. Be at ready with your blade. And you too, Short Brush! Though a child, our Rowan is vicious with her weapon."

"Yes, sire," agreed Mikkel and Short Brush.

The two grays beat the bushes in the search. Closer and closer they came to the child's hiding place, a small earthen scoop created when the roots of a wind-blown tree pulled free of the earth.

The evil lord and his lot remained mounted, ready to pursue should the young girl determine to take flight once more. And so, they were not prepared for the child's play.

Rowan softly, softly sang, "You wind-whipped branches shudder, shake. You oaks and cedars, tremble. Take these men and beasts who do us wrong. Not in these woods do they belong."

As a mighty gust of wind roared, nearby trees slapped their branches to the point of breaking, reaching out and grasping the five mounted men. An immense gaping cavern opened in the trunk of an ancient oak and swallowed the five surprised mail-clad men whole.

Mikkel and Short Brush, too, were lifted high into the air by a white pine and a blue spruce. Lifted high. Kept high. For a while.

"Return from whence you came. Go to your families, and tell them of the wrath of Sylvia," commanded Rowan. "She would not wish you to come to her land again!"

The pine and spruce tossed the two gray trackers over the trees of the forest and into the field beyond. The field was already harvested and soggy with the rains of autumn. Mikkel and Short Brush, unhurt but shaken by their arboreal flight, rose and fled immediately to tell their master of the strange doings of this wood.

GO

Name _____ Date _____

DIRECTIONS: Read the story on page 54, then answer the questions.

1. **Where do you think this story takes place? Cite evidence from the story to support your answers.**

_____

_____

_____

_____

2. **How would you describe the dialect (the way the characters talk) in this story? Based on the way the characters speak, how do you imagine they are dressed?**

_____

_____

_____

_____

3. **What details tell the reader that Rowan is very small?**

_____

_____

_____

_____

4. **What details help you picture the fierce lord?**

_____

_____

_____

_____

5. **How do you think this story would be different if it were set in a large, modern American city? Be specific.**

_____

_____

_____

_____

STOP

Effect of Technique on a Literary Work

A Doomed Romance

You are my love, my love you are.
I worship you from afar;
I through the branches spy you.

You, Sir, are a climbing thug.
I do not like your fuzzy mug.
Away from me, please take you!

Oh, grant me peace, my love, my dove.
Climb to my home so far above.
This place you call your warren.

I like my home in sheltered hollow,
Where fox and weasel may not follow.
Please go away, tree rodent!

I love your ears, so soft and tall.
I love your nose, so pink and small.
I must make you my own bride!

I will not climb, I cannot eat,
The acorns that you call a treat.
Now shimmy up that oak; hide!

Now I hide up in my bower.
Lonesome still, I shake and cower.
Sadness overtakes me.

I must stay on the lovely ground
With carrots crisp and cabbage round.
I long for gardens, not trees.

DIRECTIONS: Answer the following questions about the poem.

1. Who are the two speakers in this ballad? Identify them and write one adjective to describe the tone of each voice.

   A. _____

   _____

   B. _____

   _____

2. Briefly, what story does the poem tell? Explain in one complete sentence.

   _____

   _____

   _____

   _____

   _____

3. What do you think the theme of this poem is? Write it in one phrase or sentence.

   _____

   _____

   _____

   _____

4. Circle two adjectives to describe the first speaker in the poem.

angry	lovesick	
happy	hopeful	silly

5. Circle two adjectives to describe the second speaker in the poem.

joyful	relaxed	
annoyed	realistic	happy

6. Explain how the first speaker tries to make his home appealing to his love. Write in complete sentences.

   _____

   _____

   _____

   _____

7. Where does the second speaker live? How does it differ from where the first speaker lives? Write in complete sentences.

   _____

   _____

   _____

   _____

STOP

Character Traits

Slumber Party

It was the night Annabel had looked forward to for weeks! Four girls were arriving for a sleepover party! She had asked her parents many times, and finally they said yes.

Annabel nervously wandered around the house, waiting for her guests to arrive. Finally, four cars pulled up and the doorbell rang. Annabel threw open the door and welcomed her guests. The girls piled into Annabel's house in a jumble of sleeping bags and overnight cases.

"Thank you for inviting me," Robin replied. "I brought you a thank-you gift." She held a small box out to her hostess.

"Yum! Chocolates!" Sheila shouted. She grabbed the box and shoved a candy into her mouth. She dropped the empty wrapper on the floor. "Got any milk?" she said, with her mouth full.

"There's milk in the kitchen," Annabel said as she pointed the way. Then, she noticed that another one of her guests did not look happy. "Tamiko, what's wrong?"

"I've never slept away from home," Tamiko admitted. "I'm a little nervous. My mother said I could call home if I needed to."

"You'll be all right," Annabel reassured her. "But, you can use the phone anytime. It's right over there . . . hey? Where's the phone?" She looked at the empty table. Her eyes followed the telephone cord to a corner of the room. A girl was talking animatedly into the phone. It was the last guest, Paula.

"Is it okay if my friend Dan comes over?" Paula called over to Annabel. "He says he's bored."

"No!" Annabel responded, a little shocked. "There are no boys at this slumber party. Well, except for my kid brother, Ted."

"Oh." Paula rolled her eyes and went back to chatting on the phone.

"I brought a flashlight and a teddy bear," Tamiko showed the girls. "They'll help me feel better in the middle of the night."

"I'll put my sleeping bag next to yours," Robin told her. "I hope that makes you feel safer."

"Don't worry," Annabel smiled. "There's nothing to be afraid of!"

"Oh, yeah?" Ted chuckled to himself from his hiding place at the top of the staircase. Annabel's brother was wearing a horrible monster mask, and he carried a plastic ax. "Just wait until I jump into their room at midnight!"

GO

DIRECTIONS: Pick a word from the Word Bank to describe each of the characters. Then write two examples of behaviors from the story on the previous page that prove why your description fits each person.

Word Bank					
fearful	gracious	greedy	mischievous	polite	rude

Example:

Annabel is <u>gracious</u>.

A.   She says "Welcome!" to her guests.

B.   She shows her friends where the milk and the phone are when she's asked.

1. Robin is _____.

A.   _____

_____

B.   _____

_____

2. Sheila is _____.

A.   _____

_____

B.   _____

_____

3. Tamiko is _____.

A.   _____

_____

B.   _____

_____

4. Paula is _____.

A.   _____

_____

B.   _____

_____

5. Ted is _____.

A.   _____

_____

B.   _____

_____

STOP

Reading

Analyzing Unfamiliar Vocabulary

Read and
Understand
Literature

DIRECTIONS: Read the poem and answer the questions that follow.

Bishop Loreless

Bishop loreless,°
King redeless,°
Young men reckless,°
Old man witless
Woman shameless—
    I swear by heaven's king
    Those be five lither thing!

°*lore*—learning, knowledge
°*redeless*—without advice or guidance
°*reckless*—heedless

"Bishop Loreless" is an English poem that was written more than 600 years ago. The English language has changed quite a bit since then. Even though this poem is written in English, you are probably not familiar with some of the words. Use the mini-dictionary that accompanies the poem to help your understanding.

1. **According to the poet, it is important for all kings to have _____.**

   Ⓐ extensive landholdings

   Ⓑ wise advisors or counselors

   Ⓒ great wealth

   Ⓓ experience in battle

2. **The best definition of the word *loreless* is _____.**

   Ⓕ knowledgeable

   Ⓖ irresponsible

   Ⓗ ignorant

   Ⓙ wicked

3. **According to the poet, it is bad for which group to be irresponsible?**

   Ⓐ bishops

   Ⓑ women

   Ⓒ old men

   Ⓓ young men

4. **A definition for the phrase *lither thing* is not provided for you. Based on the rest of the poem, what do you think the phrase means?**

   Ⓕ respectable things

   Ⓖ beautiful things

   Ⓗ evil things

   Ⓙ happy things

Name _____ Date _____

Reading
2A.7

Read and
Understand
Literature

Using Comprehension Strategies

The New Vestments

By Edward Lear (1812–1888)

There lived an old man in the Kingdom of Tess,
Who invented a purely original dress;
And when it was perfectly made and complete,
He opened the door, and walked into the
street.

By way of a hat, he'd a loaf of Brown Bread,
In the middle of which he inserted his head;
His Shirt was made up of no end of dead
Mice,
The warmth of whose skins was quite fluffy
and nice;
His Drawers were of Rabbit-skins; so were
his shoes;
His Stockings were skins—but it is not known
whose;
His Waistcoat and Trousers were made up of
Pork Chops;
His Buttons were Jujubes, and Chocolate
Drops;
His coat was all Pancakes with jam for a
border,
And a girdle of Biscuits to keep him in order;
And he wore over all, as a screen from bad
weather,
A Cloak of green Cabbage-leaves stitched all
together.

He had walked a short way, when he heard a
great noise
Of all sorts of Beasticles, Birdlings, and Boys;
And from every long street and dark lane in
the town
Beasts, Birdies, and Boys in a tumult rushed
down.
Two Cows and a half ate his Cabbage-leaf
Cloak;

Four Apes seized his Girdle, which vanished
like smoke;
Three Kids ate up half of his Pancaky Coat,
And the tails were devoured by an ancient
He Goat;
An army of Dogs in a twinkling tore up his
Pork Waistcoat and Trousers to give to their
Puppies;
And while they were growling, and mumbling
the Chops,
Ten Boys prigged the Jujubes and Chocolate
Drops.
He tried to run back to his house, but in vain,
For Scores of fat Pigs came again and again;
They rushed out of stables and hovels and
doors,
They tore off his stockings, his shoes, and his
drawers;
And now from the housetops with screechings
descend,
Striped, spotted, white, black, and gray Cats
without end,
They jumped on his shoulders and knocked
off his hat,

When Crows, Ducks, and Hens made a
mincemeat of that,
They speedily flew at his sleeves in a trice,
And utterly tore up his Shirt of dead Mice;
They swallowed the last of his Shirt with a
squall,
Whereon he ran home with no clothes on
at all.

And he said to himself as he bolted the door,
"I will not wear a similar dress anymore,
Anymore, anymore, anymore, nevermore!"

Name _____ Date _____

DIRECTIONS: Using the poem map below, highlight the key story elements in this silly poem.

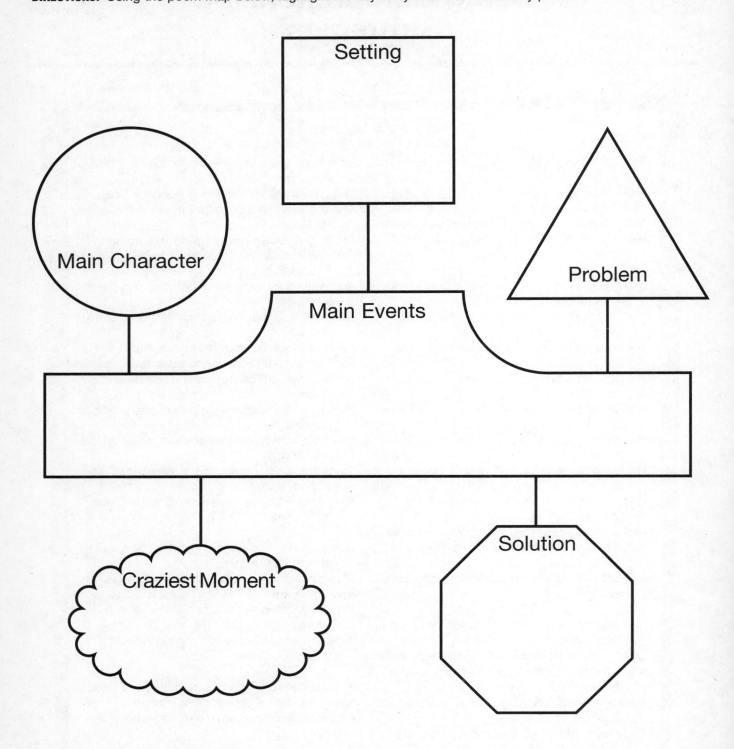

Setting

Main Character

Problem

Main Events

Craziest Moment

Solution

STOP

Reading

2A.8

Read and Understand Literature

Differences Between Fiction and Nonfiction

DIRECTIONS: Read the passages. Then in each of the lists, circle the characteristics that you think are true about each passage.

Hibernation

Have you ever wondered why some animals hibernate? Hibernation is when animals sleep through the winter. Animals get their warmth and energy from food. Some animals cannot find enough food in the winter, so they must eat large amounts of food in the fall. Their bodies store this food as fat. Then in winter, they hibernate and their bodies live on the stored fat. Since their bodies need much less food during hibernation, they can stay alive without eating new food during the winter. Some animals that hibernate are bats, chipmunks, bears, snakes, and turtles.

Waterland

"Hurray!" cried Meghan. "Today is the day we're going to Waterland!" It was a hot July day, and Meghan's mom was taking her and her new friend Jake.

Just then, Meghan's mom came out of her bedroom. She did not look very happy. "What's the matter, Mom? Are you afraid to get wet?" Meghan teased.

Mrs. Millett told the kids that she wasn't felling well. She was too tired to drive to the water park.

Meghan and Jake were disappointed. "My mom has chronic fatigue syndrome," Meghan explained. "Her illness makes her really tired. She's still a great mom."

"Thank you, dear," said Mrs. Millett. "I'm too tired to drive, but I have an idea. You can make your own Waterland, and I'll rest in the lawn chair."

Meghan and Jake set up three different sprinklers. They dragged the play slide over to the wading pool and aimed the sprinkler on the slide. Meghan and Jake got soaking wet and played all day.

"Thank you for being so understanding," Meghan's mom said. "Now I feel better, but I'm really hot! There's only one cure for that." She stood under the sprinkler with all her clothes on. She was drenched from head to toe.

Meghan laughed and said, "Now you have chronic wet syndrome." Mrs. Millett rewarded her daughter with a big, wet hug.

Hibernation

Includes facts and opinions

Made up or fantasized

Main purpose is to inform

Main purpose is to entertain

Organized into setting, characters, problem, goal, events, and resolution

Organized according to the purpose the authors wish to achieve (steps to achieve a goal; explain why something happens; attempt to make an argument; etc.)

Waterland

Includes facts and opinions

Made up or fantasized

Main purpose is to inform

Main purpose is to entertain

Organized into setting, characters, problem, goal, events, and resolution

Organized according to the purpose the authors wish to achieve (steps to achieve a goal; explain why something happens; attempt to make an argument; etc.)

Name _____ Date _____

Reading
2A
For pages 53–63

Read and
Understand
Literature

Mini-Test 4

One Afternoon in March

One afternoon in March, I went for a walk. After being cooped up all winter, it felt good to wander around outside. I was walking down the street when something caught my eye. I leaned down and found two silver dollars shining in a half-melted snow bank. *Buried treasure!* was my first thought. So, I dug through the snow looking for more. I slipped the two coins into my pocket and went home colder but richer. I began to think about how to spend the money. I could add it to my skateboard fund. Or I could use it to buy a soda and hot pretzel, my favorite snack. The possibilities were exciting.

Two days later, my friend Mary Ann and her little sister were searching the snow banks. *Finders keepers*, I thought. I didn't need to get to the *losers weepers* part since Susy was already crying for real.

"I dropped them right here," she said between tears. Her hands were cold and red from digging in the snow.

"Maybe they got shoved down the street with the snow plow. Let's dig over here." Mary Ann's voice sounded optimistic.

"Phil, have you seen two silver dollars?" asked Mary Ann. Susy looked up from digging. Her eyes were hopeful.

"Coins?" I said.

"Yeah, Susy dropped two silver dollars along here last week."

"Silver dollars?"

"Yeah," said Susy. "They're thick and big." She brushed the snow off her red hands and wiped the tears from her face. Her eyes were as red as her hands.

"As a matter of fact," I hesitated, "I dug two coins out of that snow bank just a few days ago. I wondered who might have lost them."

Susy leaped on me, hugging me. "Oh, thank you, thank you."

DIRECTIONS: Answer the following questions.

1. Name the characters in the story.

_____

_____

2. Who is narrating the story?

_____

_____

3. What is the setting?

_____

_____

4. What is the problem in the story?

- (A) Susy has lost two silver dollars.
- (B) Phil won't give up the coins he found.
- (C) Phil doesn't want to help Susy find her coins.
- (D) Mary Ann doesn't want to help her sister.

5. Which of the following best describes the narrator of this story?

- (F) devious
- (G) honest
- (H) jovial
- (J) deceitful

Reading Standards

Read and Understand Literature

Goal 2: Read and understand literature representative of various societies, eras, and ideas.

Learning Standard 2A *(See page 52.)*

Learning Standard 2B—Students who meet the standard can read and interpret a variety of literary works.

1. Create an extension to a literary text (e.g., alternate ending, additional dialog for a character). *(See page 66.)*
2. Make inferences, draw conclusions, and make connections from text to text, text to self, and text to world. *(See page 67.)*
3. Analyze and remedy difficulties in comprehension (e.g., questioning, rephrasing, analyzing). *(See pages 68–69.)*
4. Compare ideas from texts representing a variety of times and cultures. *(See page 70.)*
5. Make inferences and draw conclusions about contexts, events, character, and settings. *(See page 71.)*
6. Read a wide range of nonfiction (e.g., books, newspapers, magazines, textbooks, visual media). *(See page 72.)*
7. Support plausible interpretations with evidence from the text. *(See page 73.)*

Reading
| 2B.1 |

Creating an Extension to a Story

DIRECTIONS: Read the story. Then make up an additional part to the story (extra dialog for a character, a different ending, etc.) and write it in the space provided.

Cyber Love

Alex sat next to the girl of his dreams every day in science, math, and computer applications. Every day CeCe smiled at Alex with her pretty, silver smile. Like Alex, she wore braces. She wrote notes to him during class and laughed at all his jokes. Alex thought she liked him, but he was too shy to ask. He worried that the year would pass without ever learning for certain.

When Valentine's Day approached, Alex thought he had a chance. He would send her a special valentine. Unfortunately, he had no money. He was desperate, so desperate that he broke down and talked to his dad.

When Alex's dad said, "Try cyberspace," Alex was confused. He wondered how the Internet could help him. But when he visited the Free Virtual Valentine Web site, he knew his problem was solved. He chose a musical valentine and e-mailed it to CeCe at school.

On Valentine's Day, Alex waited patiently for CeCe to open her e-mail. He tried to look busy as he watched her out of the corner of his eye. CeCe whispered, "You sent me a message," as she clicked on the hot link to Alex's valentine. Then she turned to Alex and said, "You're great."

I'm great, Alex thought to himself. *She likes me. If only I'd discovered cyberspace a long time ago.*

_____

_____

_____

_____

_____

_____

_____

_____

_____

_____

_____

Inferencing/Drawing Conclusions

The North Star

The North Star is one of the most famous stars. Its star name is *Polaris.* It is called the North Star because it shines almost directly over the North Pole. If you are at the North Pole, the North Star is overhead. As you travel farther south, the star seems lower in the sky. Only people in the Northern Hemisphere can see the North Star.

Because the North Star is always in the same spot in the sky, it has been used for years to give direction to people at night. Sailors used the North Star to navigate through the oceans.

Polaris, like all stars, is always moving. Thousands of years from now, another star will get to be the North Star. Vega was the North Star thousands of years before it moved out of position and Polaris became the North Star.

DIRECTIONS: Answer the questions based on the passage.

1. **The North Star might be one of the most famous stars because _____ .**
   - (A) it is near the North Pole
   - (B) it is always moving
   - (C) it is always in the same spot in the sky
   - (D) it is difficult to find in the sky

2. **Another star will someday get to be the North Star because _____ .**
   - (F) stars are always moving
   - (G) there are many stars in the sky
   - (H) Earth will turn to the South Pole
   - (J) scientists rename it every 50 years

3. **The name Polaris most likely comes from which name?**
   - (A) polecat
   - (B) polar bear
   - (C) Poland
   - (D) North Pole

4. **If you step outside tonight and see Polaris in the sky, that will prove that you are in the _____ Hemisphere.**
   - (F) Eastern
   - (G) Western
   - (H) Northern
   - (J) Southern

STOP

Name _____   Date _____

Reading

2B.3

Read and
Understand
Literature

Remedying Difficulties in Comprehension

Go, Man, Go!

They stretched in midfield, preparing for the morning's events. Ted, dressed in the red and white of his school, worked alongside the rest of the seventeen athletes who had come to the meet from Weston Middle School.

Theo was hardworking, and he had trained well. Since the snow thawed in early March, he had kept his disciplined regiments of warm-up, long run, sprints, and cooldown. As the weeks passed, he settled into a daily four-mile run. The first few times were painful. His side ached, his calves tightened, his right knee flared, and his forehead burned. On those nights, he would flop down on his bed and sleep soundly without even undressing.

Now, on this warm and bright May morning, it was time to prove his worth, and Theo found he was very nervous. Twenty-two schools were participating in the invitational meet. The field was spangled with athletes whose school-colored clothes offered a visual display of diversity. Weston's girls had already scored points in the long jump and javelin. The boys had done well, too. Theo's high jump had won his school a second place. They also had a second and fourth in the pole vault. Not bad, considering that track and field was a brand new sport to Weston Middle School.

Theo's main event was the 400-meter dash. It was what he dreamed of running ever since he saw his Uncle Dave's victorious sprint seven years ago. Yet, these meets made Theo so nervous, he often wished he were sacked out in front of the television instead. As he pranced about, shaking away the jitters, Theo saw a lone figure at the long-jump pit. He was a thin, dark boy roughly Theo's height and build. He wore the only gray T-shirt in the wild mass of school colors. Even though he looked out of place, the boy seemed calm and sure of himself. Theo crossed over to the pit. He introduced himself to the runner, a friendly, determined student named Carl Alvarez. Carl was the only entrant from his school. He had taken two city buses to get there, and he was there just for the 400-meter race. Like Theo, this was his first year in track and field. Carl didn't seem fazed by his solitary status, though. He told Theo he wanted to help form a team at his school. Returning to his own gathered team, Theo admitted to himself that Carl's attitude was impressive.

When the 400 was announced and Theo lined up, the Weston team set up a chant. Theo glanced at Carl, who didn't have anyone to cheer for him, but Carl seemed focused and ready for his race. As the pistol fired, Theo shot out. The full field of runners—eight boys in eight lanes—swarmed down the stretch. The Weston team yelled, "Go, man, go!" Every Weston student screamed as Theo's lead became evident coming out of the first curve.

Theo's heart pounded as he crossed over to the inside lane. He was leading! Footsteps thudded behind him as he entered the wide, dangerous final turn. Someone was pulling alongside him. It was Carl! They glanced at each other briefly. Then they focused. Theo looked ahead and smiled grimly. Okay, let's race, he thought. Around the curve he ran, Carl at his side matching him step for step, yet never falling back. The two boys sped into the final stretch. Theo raced as never before, neck to neck with his challenger.

Name _____ Date _____

DIRECTIONS: Improve your comprehension of the story on the previous page by filling in the character web.

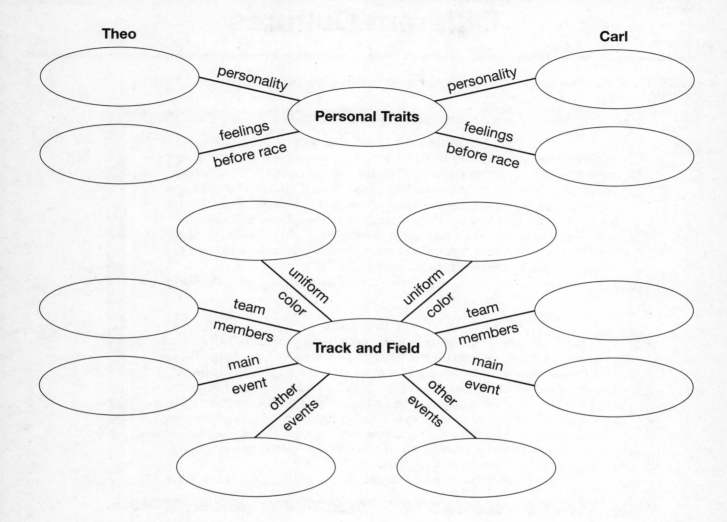

Theo

Carl

personality

personality

Personal Traits

feelings

feelings

before race

before race

uniform color

uniform color

team members

team members

Track and Field

main event

main event

other events

other events

DIRECTIONS: The setting for *Go, Man, Go!* has lots of detail. Find these details in the story.

1. **How many schools were at the meet?**

_____

2. **What created so much color on the field?**

_____

3. **How long had Theo been training?**

_____

4. **In what month does this story take place?**

_____

5. **Describe the weather on the day of the meet.**

_____

6. **How many runners start the 400-meter dash?**

_____

STOP

Name _____ Date _____

Reading
2B.4

Read and
Understand
Literature

Comparing Texts From Different Cultures

DIRECTIONS: Read the passage and answer the questions that follow.

Walks All Over the Sky

Back when the sky was completely dark, there was a chief with two sons, a younger son, *One Who Walks All Over the Sky,* and an older son, *Walking About Early.* The younger son was sad to see the sky always so dark, so he made a mask out of wood and pitch (the sun) and lit it on fire. Each day, he travels across the sky. At night, he sleeps below the horizon and when he snores sparks fly from the mask and make the stars. The older brother became jealous. To impress their father, he smeared fat and charcoal on his face (the moon) and makes his own path across the sky.

–From the *Tsimshian of the Pacific Northwest*

The Porcupine

Once Porcupine and Beaver argued about the seasons. Porcupine wanted five winter months. He held up one hand and showed his five fingers. He said, "Let the winter months be the same in number as the fingers on my hand." Beaver said, "No," and held up his tail, which had many cracks or scratches on it. He said, "Let the winter months be the same in number as the scratches on my tail." They argued more, and Porcupine got angry and bit off his thumb. Then, holding up his hand with the four fingers, he said, "There must be only four winter months." Beaver was afraid and gave in. For this reason, today porcupines have four claws on each foot.

–From the *Tahltan: Teit, Journal of American Folk-Lore,* xxxii, 226

Both of these stories are from different cultures. However, they both try to explain something.

1. **What is explained in the first story?**

   _____

   _____

2. **What is explained in the second story?**

   _____

   _____

3. **Who are the two characters in the first story? In the second story?**

   _____

   _____

4. **How is the relationship between the characters in the first story and the characters in the second story alike?**

   _____

   _____

   _____

Reading

2B.5

Inferencing/Drawing Conclusions

**Read and
Understand
Literature**

DIRECTIONS: Read the passage and answer the questions that follow.

Example:

Police officers carry equipment that helps them to protect themselves and other people. They carry guns, nightsticks, flashlights, and handcuffs on their belts. Some wear bullet-proof vests. They also carry two-way radios so they can call other officers for assistance.

A. Why would police officers need equipment for protection?

- (A) because they teach people about the laws
- (B) because they are trained to use the equipment
- (C) because sometimes their work can be dangerous
- (D) because they need to write reports

Answer: (C)

I was so nervous. I hadn't seen Abbie in three years, not since my mom got that new job. I remember the day we moved away. Abbie brought me our photograph in a frame. I gave her a necklace with a friendship charm on it. We promised to stay friends forever. Now that I was finally going to see her again, I wondered if we would still like the same kinds of things and laugh at the same kinds of jokes. I rubbed my sweaty palms on my jeans as we pulled into Abbie's driveway.

1. Why hasn't the narrator seen Abbie for three years?

- (A) They were best friends.
- (B) They didn't like each other's gifts.
- (C) They had a fight.
- (D) The narrator had to move away.

2. Why are the narrator's palms sweaty?

- (F) She is nervous.
- (G) She has a fever.
- (H) She feels sick.
- (J) She doesn't want to move.

3. The passage gives you enough information to believe that the narrator _____ .

- (A) was angry at her mom for making her move
- (B) had a special friendship with Abbie
- (C) liked her new school
- (D) doesn't keep her promises

4. The narrator will feel happy if _____ .

- (F) Abbie is not home
- (G) Abbie has changed a lot
- (H) she gets to move again
- (J) she and Abbie still get along

Reading

Reading a Wide Range of Nonfiction

DIRECTIONS: The passages below are either from a newspaper, an instruction manual, a textbook, or a biography. Read the passages, then identify the source of each.

1. The best way to understand the food web is to study a model of it. Refer to Figure 2.3 to see a model of a food web in a deciduous forest. Recall that in Chapter 1 we identified animals as either herbivores, carnivores, or omnivores. Which animals in Figure 2.3 could best be described as herbivores?

   _____

2. LONDON, England—Buckingham Palace announced today that Queen Elizabeth will make a short visit to the United States early next week to attend the annual Westhampton Flower Show in Westhampton, Connecticut. The Queen has made several trips to the flower show, often accompanied by other members of the royal family. Last year the prize-winning rose at the show was named in honor of the Queen.

   _____

3. Wolfgang Amadeus Mozart was born on January 27,1756, in Austria. When he was just three years old, he learned to play the harpsichord. He was composing music by the time he was five years old. At the age of six, he was invited to perform for the Empress of Austria. Mozart astonished people with his musical ability. He was called a child genius.

   _____

4. Step 1: Find Pieces A, B, and C and Main Frame 1.
   Step 2: Insert Piece A into the square slot on Piece B.
   Step 3: Insert Piece C into the round slot on Piece B.
   Step 4: Snap the assembled ABC assembly into Main Frame 1.

DIRECTIONS: Based on the titles below, identify the form of nonfiction of each.

5. *Sports Weekly*
   - (A) magazine
   - (B) textbook
   - (C) essay
   - (D) reference book

6. *Dinner in Under an Hour*
   - (F) newspaper
   - (G) cookbook
   - (H) science journal
   - (J) computer manual

STOP

Reading

2B.7

Interpreting a Text

DIRECTIONS: Read the passage and answer the questions that follow.

It's as black as ink out here in the pasture, and I'm as tired as an old shoe. But even if I were in my bed, I don't think I'd be sleeping like a baby tonight.

Last summer for my birthday, my parents gave me my dream horse. Her name is Goldie. She is a beautiful palomino. I love to watch her gallop around the pasture. She runs like the wind and looks so carefree. I hope I'll see her run that way again.

Yesterday, after I fed her, I forgot to close the door to the feed shed. She got into the grain and ate like a pig, which is very unhealthy for a horse. The veterinarian said I have to watch her like a hawk tonight to be sure she doesn't get colic. That's a very bad stomachache. Because he also said I should keep her moving, I have walked her around and around the pasture until I feel like we're on a merry-go-round.

Now the sun is finally beginning to peek over the horizon, and Goldie seems content. I think she's going to be as good as new.

1. **What will the narrator most likely do the next time she feeds the horse?**

   Ⓐ She will feed the horse too much.

   Ⓑ She will make sure she closes the feed shed door.

   Ⓒ She will give the horse plenty of water.

   Ⓓ She will leave the feed shed open.

2. **How much experience do you think the narrator has with horses?**

   Ⓕ Lots. She's probably owned many horses before.

   Ⓖ This is probably her first horse. She doesn't have a lot of experience.

   Ⓗ She's probably owned a horse before this, but not many.

   Ⓙ I can't tell from the story.

3. **Based on the passage, which of the following is most likely true about the narrator?**

   Ⓐ She really does not care much about Goldie.

   Ⓑ She is devoted to Goldie and will be dedicated to helping her.

   Ⓒ She will not want to have anything to do with horses in the future.

   Ⓓ The story does not reveal anything about the narrator.

4. **Write a line or two from the passage to support your answer to question 3.**

   _____

   _____

   _____

STOP

Name _____ Date _____

Reading

2B

For pages 66–73

Read and
Understand
Literature

Mini-Test 5

DIRECTIONS: Read each passage. Fill in the circle next to the answer you think is correct.

It was Saturday morning. All the world was smiling and bright—all, that is, except Tom Sawyer. With his pail of whitewash and a large brush, Tom stared sadly at the long fence. He dipped his brush into the white glop and began the job of whitewashing the fence.

1. **This passage tells us about a boy named Tom Sawyer. How does Tom feel about whitewashing the fence?**

   Ⓐ glum

   Ⓑ joyful

   Ⓒ excited

   Ⓓ cheerful

Misha stood on the stage. His hands shook so hard that he could barely hold his violin. A hush fell over the audience. He shut his eyes tight and remembered what his music teacher had told him: "You can do it. Take a deep breath and pretend that you're standing in your living room." Misha lifted his violin to his chin and played his solo perfectly from beginning to end.

2. **From this passage, what do you know about Misha?**

   Ⓕ He has been playing the violin for many years.

   Ⓖ He gets nervous when he is performing in front of others.

   Ⓗ He likes to play his violin in front of an audience.

   Ⓙ He and his music teacher are friends.

DIRECTIONS: Reread the story about Misha in question 3. Then write an additional paragraph describing what happens after Misha plays his violin solo.

3. _____

   _____

   _____

   _____

   _____

   _____

   _____

   _____

   _____

   _____

   _____

   _____

STOP

74

How Am I Doing?

Mini-Test 1

Page 17

Number Correct

8–9 answers correct	**Great Job!** Move on to the section test on page 77.
5–7 answers correct	**You're almost there!** But you still need a little practice. Review practice pages 8–16 before moving on to the section test on page 77.
0–4 answers correct	**Oops!** Time to review what you have learned and try again. Review the practice section on pages 8–16. Then retake the test on page 17. Now move on to the section test on page 77.

Mini-Test 2

Page 33

Number Correct

4 answers correct	**Awesome!** Move on to the section test on page 77.
3 answers correct	**You're almost there!** But you still need a little practice. Review practice pages 19–32 before moving on to the section test on page 77.
0–2 answers correct	**Oops!** Time to review what you have learned and try again. Review the practice section on pages 19–32. Then retake the test on page 33. Now move on to the section test on page 77.

Mini-Test 3

Page 50

Number Correct

6 answers correct	**Great Job!** Move on to the section test on page 77.
4–5 answers correct	**You're almost there!** But you still need a little practice. Review practice pages 35–49 before moving on to the section test on page 77.
0–3 answers correct	**Oops!** Time to review what you have learned and try again. Review the practice section on pages 35–49. Then retake the test on page 50. Now move on to the section test on page 77.

How Am I Doing?

Mini-Test 4	5 answers correct	**Awesome!** Move on to the section test on page 77.
Page 64 **Number Correct**	3–4 answers correct	**You're almost there!** But you still need a little practice. Review practice pages 53–63 before moving on to the section test on page 77.
	0–2 answers correct	**Oops!** Time to review what you have learned and try again. Review the practice section on pages 53–63. Then retake the test on page 64. Now move on to the section test on page 77.
Mini-Test 5	4 answers correct	**Great Job!** Move on to the section test on page 77.
Page 74 **Number Correct**	3 answers correct	**You're almost there!** But you still need a little practice. Review practice pages 66–73 before moving on to the section test on page 77.
	0–2 answers correct	**Oops!** Time to review what you have learned and try again. Review the practice section on pages 66–73. Then retake the test on page 74. Now move on to the section test on page 77.

Final Reading Test
for pages 8–74

DIRECTIONS: Choose the best answer.

1. Which of these words probably comes from the Latin word *binioculus* meaning "two eyes at a time"?

    (A) bindery

    (B) bingo

    (C) binoculars

    (D) binomial

2. If *prae* means "in front of" or "before" in Latin, then which of these words probably means taking care before doing something?

    (F) precaution

    (G) product

    (H) pressure

    (J) preserve

DIRECTIONS: Choose the word that means the same or about the same as the underlined word.

3. a bundle of goods

    (A) sweater

    (B) burden

    (C) rumble

    (D) package

4. restore the wood

    (F) repair

    (G) retread

    (H) relieve

    (J) reduce

5. The dishes clattered in the sink.

    (A) rattled

    (B) broke

    (C) jumped

    (D) washed

DIRECTIONS: Choose the word that means the opposite of the underlined word.

6. contemporary art

    (F) modern

    (G) ancient

    (H) imaginative

    (J) folksy

7. scamper away

    (A) waltz

    (B) crawl

    (C) stroll

    (D) sprint

8. reckless behavior

    (F) foolish

    (G) carefree

    (H) juvenile

    (J) thoughtful

9. the collapse of the government

    (A) creation

    (B) structure

    (C) downfall

    (D) laws

DIRECTIONS: Read the sentences. Choose the word that correctly completes both sentences

10. The dog caught the _____ .

    Our school has a formal _____ .

    (F) ball

    (G) dance

    (H) stick

    (J) event

GO

11. The _____ climbed the tree.

I can't _____ this heat.

- Ⓐ fox
- Ⓑ stand
- Ⓒ cat
- Ⓓ bear

DIRECTIONS: Read the passage and answer the questions that follow.

Easter Island

Few places in the world are more intriguing and mystifying than Easter Island, located in the Pacific Ocean 2,300 miles from the coast of Chile. Easter Island has 64 square miles of rugged coastline and steep hills. Scientists believe the island began as a volcano. Three extinct volcanoes remain on the island. The largest one rises 1,400 feet high.

On Easter Sunday of 1722, Dutch Admiral Jacob Roggeveen and his crew landed on Easter Island aboard the Dutch ship *Arena*. The astonished crew found dozens of huge stone figures standing on long stone platforms. The statues, some measuring 40 feet tall, were similar in appearance. Their expressionless faces were without eyes. Huge red stone cylinders were placed on their heads. Since that time, the island has been a source of mystery and intrigue to scientists and explorers.

Archaeologists believe that three different cultures lived on Easter Island. Around 400 A.D., the island was inhabited by a group of people who specialized in making small stone statues.

Years later, another civilization tore down these statues and used them to build long temple platforms called *ahus*. These people carved more than 600 enormous stone busts of human forms and placed them on the *ahus*. Some *ahus* still hold up to 15 statues.

Scientists believe that the statues were carved from hard volcanic rock in the crater walls of the volcano called *Rana Raraku*. The statues were chiseled with stone picks made of basalt. Although the statues weigh many tons each, it is believed that they were moved with ropes and rollers across the island and placed on the *ahus*. This may be the reason for one island legend about the statues "walking" to their site.

About 1670, another group of people invaded the island. These invaders practiced cannibalism. During this time, many people began living in underground caves where they hid their treasures.

Today, Easter Island is governed by Chile, a country of South America. Almost the entire population of 2,000 people live in the small village of Hanga Roa on the west coast of the island.

12. The author's purpose in writing this passage is most likely _____ .

- Ⓕ to convince readers to visit Easter Island
- Ⓖ to tell about a trip to Easter Island
- Ⓗ to explain why Easter Island is a source of mystery
- Ⓙ to report the latest scientific findings about Easter Island

13. The author believes that Easter Island is _____ .

- Ⓐ fascinating to study
- Ⓑ not worth scientific study
- Ⓒ not a real place
- Ⓓ the result of cannibalism

14. According to the author, which of the following is true about *ahus*?

- Ⓕ People who lived in underground caves built the *ahus*.
- Ⓖ *Ahus* were chiseled with stone picks.
- Ⓗ There is no such thing as *ahus*.
- Ⓙ It is likely that ropes and rollers moved the statues to the *ahus*.

15. Which words most clearly reveal the author's feelings about the subject of Easter Island?

- Ⓐ intriguing and mystifying
- Ⓑ silly and unimportant
- Ⓒ rugged coastline
- Ⓓ enormous stone

DIRECTIONS: Read the passage and answer the questions that follow.

The Story of Arachne

Long ago in a far away country lived a young woman named Arachne. She was not rich or beautiful, but she had one great talent. Arachne could weave the most beautiful cloth anyone had ever seen. Everyone in Arachne's village talked about her wonderful cloth, and soon she became famous. But as her fame grew, so did her pride.

GO

"No one else can weave as well as I can," Arachne boasted. "Not even the goddess Minerva could make anything so lovely and fine."

Now Minerva wove cloth for all the gods. She was proud of her weaving too and thought that no human being could ever match her skills. Soon Arachne's words reached Minerva's ears, and the goddess became angry.

"So the human woman thinks she is better than I!" Minerva roared. "We will see about that!"

Minerva searched the countryside until she came upon Arachne's home. Minerva called to Arachne and challenged her to a contest. "Let us both weave a length of cloth. We will see whose is the most beautiful."

Arachne agreed. She set up two looms, and she and Minerva went to work. The goddess wove cloth of all the colors of the rainbow. It sparkled in the sun and floated on the breeze like a butterfly. But Arachne wove cloth that sparkled like gold and jewels. The villagers were dazzled by Arachne's cloth. When Minerva inspected it, she knew Arachne was the best weaver.

Minerva was enraged. She took out a jar of magic water and sprinkled it on Arachne. Instantly, poor Arachne began to change. She shrank smaller and smaller until she could almost not be seen. She grew more arms and became covered in fine brown hair. When it was all over, Arachne had become a tiny brown spider. Arachne would never boast again, but she would spend the rest of her life weaving fine webs.

16. People in ancient times made up stories, or myths, to explain things in their world that they did not understand. This myth explains _____ .

- (F) how to weave cloth
- (G) why spiders weave webs
- (H) how to turn a person into a spider
- (J) why it is wrong to be boastful

17. What might have happened if Arachne had not bragged about her talents?

- (A) Minerva would have left her alone.
- (B) Arachne would not have become famous.
- (C) The villagers would not have appreciated Arachne's weaving.
- (D) Minerva would not be allowed to make cloth for the gods anymore.

18. What caused Minerva to challenge Arachne to the contest?

- (F) boredom and skill
- (G) contentment and humility
- (H) fear and confusion
- (J) pride and jealousy

19. This passage tells us the most about the _____ .

- (A) plot
- (B) mood
- (C) characters
- (D) setting

20. This story might have been told to remind people not to _____ .

- (F) brag about their talents
- (G) weave cloth
- (H) enter competitions
- (J) kill spiders

DIRECTIONS: Read the paragraph. Choose the word that best fits in each numbered blank.

The armadillo is (21)_____ in several ways. First, the female gives birth to four babies, and they are always the same sex. Second, when an armadillo is (22)_____ and cannot escape to its (23)_____ or quickly dig itself into the ground, it rolls itself into a tight, protective ball. This is possible because of the joined (24)_____ plates of its shell. The armadillo also tucks in its head and feet. If, by chance, it (25)_____ to reach the safety of its burrow, the armadillo can hold on so tightly with its strong claws that it is virtually impossible to pull it out.

21.
- (A) honored
- (B) unusual
- (C) motivated
- (D) typical

GO

22.
- (F) assisted
- (G) free
- (H) cornered
- (J) released

23.
- (A) burrow
- (B) vehicle
- (C) porch
- (D) dormitory

24.
- (F) overlapping
- (G) detached
- (H) soft
- (J) disconnected

25.
- (A) endeavors
- (B) insists
- (C) actually
- (D) manages

DIRECTIONS: Read the passage and answer the questions that follow.

There are many differences between frogs and toads. Frogs have narrow bodies and ridges down their backs. They have large, round ear membranes and small teeth in their upper jaws. Their long hind legs **enable** them to take long leaps. They have smooth, moist, soft skin. Most frogs are water-dwellers. They lay clumps of eggs in their watery habitat.

In contrast, toads have chubby bodies and ridges on their heads. Toads make their homes on land, and their skin is thick, dry, and bumpy. A toad's short legs **limit** it to short leaps only. Their ear membranes are smaller. They have no teeth. Although toads are land-dwellers, they deposit their eggs in water as frogs do. However, they lay eggs in strings rather than clumps.

26. What would be a good title for this passage?
- (F) "Laying Eggs in Water"
- (G) "Frogs and Toads: What's the Difference?"
- (H) "Amphibians"
- (J) "Similarities Between Frogs and Toads"

27. In this passage, the word *limit* means _____.
- (A) to restrict or hold back
- (B) boundary
- (C) the greatest number or amount allowed
- (D) ultimate

28. Which word is an antonym for *enable*?
- (F) prevent
- (G) assist
- (H) inedible
- (J) teach

29. Which of the following is not a fact?
- (A) Toads have chubbier bodies than frogs.
- (B) Frogs have longer hind legs than toads.
- (C) Toads have smaller ear membranes than frogs.
- (D) Frogs are more attractive than toads.

DIRECTIONS: Read the passage and answer the questions that follow.

To pay off its national debts, the British government increased the taxes paid on its products by its colonists. The American colonists thought this was very unfair. They protested by throwing British tea and merchandise into Boston Harbor.

30. Why did the American colonists throw tea into Boston Harbor?
- (F) The British had too many debts.
- (G) They wanted coffee instead of tea.
- (H) They didn't like tea.
- (J) They thought the tax increase was unfair.

31. This passage belongs to which genre?
- (A) fable
- (B) drama
- (C) biography
- (D) historical narrative

Name _____ Date _____

Reading Test
Answer Sheet

1 (A) (B) (C) (D)
2 (F) (G) (H) (J)
3 (A) (B) (C) (D)
4 (F) (G) (H) (J)
5 (A) (B) (C) (D)
6 (F) (G) (H) (J)
7 (A) (B) (C) (D)
8 (F) (G) (H) (J)
9 (A) (B) (C) (D)
10 (F) (G) (H) (J)

11 (A) (B) (C) (D)
12 (F) (G) (H) (J)
13 (A) (B) (C) (D)
14 (F) (G) (H) (J)
15 (A) (B) (C) (D)
16 (F) (G) (H) (J)
17 (A) (B) (C) (D)
18 (F) (G) (H) (J)
19 (A) (B) (C) (D)
20 (F) (G) (H) (J)

21 (A) (B) (C) (D)
22 (F) (G) (H) (J)
23 (A) (B) (C) (D)
24 (F) (G) (H) (J)
25 (A) (B) (C) (D)
26 (F) (G) (H) (J)
27 (A) (B) (C) (D)
28 (F) (G) (H) (J)
29 (A) (B) (C) (D)
30 (F) (G) (H) (J)

31 (A) (B) (C) (D)

Writing Standards

Write to Communicate

Goal 3: Write to communicate for a variety of purposes.

Learning Standard 3A—Students who meet the standard can use correct grammar, spelling, punctuation, capitalization, and structure.

1. Write paragraphs that include a variety of sentence types (i.e., declarative, interrogative, exclamatory, imperative). *(See page 83.)*
2. Develop multi-paragraph compositions that include an introduction, first and second level support, and a conclusion. *(See page 84.)*
3. Use a variety of sentence structures (e.g., simple, compound). *(See page 85.)*
4. Use basic transition words to connect ideas. *(See page 86.)*
5. Proofread for correct English conventions. *(See page 87.)*
6. Demonstrate appropriate use of various parts of speech. *(See page 88.)*

Learning Standard 3B *(See page 90.)*

Learning Standard 3C *(See page 102.)*

Writing

3A.1

Write to
Communicate

Using a Variety of Sentence Types

A *declarative* sentence makes a statement: Ben walked home from school with Jaime.

An *interrogative* sentence asks a question: Will you feed the fish today?

An *exclamatory* sentence shows excitement or emotion: Hey! Stop hitting me!

An *imperative* sentence expresses a command or request: Come to the principal's office now.

DIRECTIONS: Below are eight short paragraphs. For each paragraph, underline the declarative sentences. Then in each blank, write IN if the paragraph also contains an interrogative sentence; write EX if it contains an exclamatory sentence; write IM if it contains an imperative sentence; write NONE if it contains only declarative sentences.

1. _____ **You are on a deserted island: no town, no people—just you and those crazy, noisy seagulls. What are you going to do?**

2. _____ **Toward the castle she fled. She begged the gatekeeper for entrance. He was as deaf as a gargoyle. He did not hear her cries. Past the stone walls she scurried, the hounds in pursuit.**

3. _____ **Maggie bit her lip. No use crying about it. She pulled her math homework out of the sink and just stared at her little sister.**

4. _____ **The music is playing those lovely Christmas tunes, but you're not listening. You can't. You have too many important things to plan. What should you buy for Teddie? Who should you invite to the party? And . . .**

5. _____ **I'm not proud of it. Really, I am not. But no teacher's ever gotten through to me. I guess I'm just not cut out to be a scholar.**

6. _____ **Columbus stood on the deck of the ship. Land was on the horizon. Land! Not the edge of the world, not dragons to devour the ship, but the land that would make his fortune . . . his and Spain's.**

7. _____ **I think Mama forgot me. Otherwise, she would come and find me. Oh, no! I've been bad! Mama said not to go see the toys because I'd get lost. Mama is going to be mad at me!**

8. _____ **Do not stop reading until you reach the end of this story. What you are about to read is so amazing that you simply *must* hear about it now. So settle back and get ready for the most incredible tale you've ever heard.**

DIRECTIONS: In the space below, write two short paragraphs on topics of your choice. Use all four sentence types at least once in the paragraphs.

9. _____

_____

_____

10. _____

_____

_____

STOP

Name _____ Date _____

Developing Compositions

DIRECTIONS: Write three short paragraphs about what you could do around your neighborhood to make money. Structure your composition as follows:

Paragraph 1: Pick one thing you could do around your neighborhood to make money. Describe what you would do.

Paragraph 2: Give two reasons why your neighbors should hire you to do this for them.

Paragraph 3: Conclude by convincing your neighbors to hire you.

_____

_____

_____

_____

_____

_____

_____

_____

_____

_____

_____

_____

_____

_____

_____

_____

_____

_____

_____

_____

Name _____ Date _____

Write to Communicate

Using a Variety of Sentence Structures

DIRECTIONS: Rewrite each run-on sentence to make it correct. Write *C* if the sentences below are correct as is.

1. Let's ask David to come with us. He knows about a great bike trail.

_____

_____

2. I can ride faster than you can let's race to the stop sign.

_____

_____

3. I'm thirsty does anyone have some bottled water?

_____

_____

4. We need to be careful on the bike trail in-line skaters can appear fast.

_____

_____

5. Do you know how to recognize a happy bicyclist? He has bugs in his teeth.

_____

_____

6. I love the playground it has great swings.

_____

_____

7. When I swing too high, I get sick do you?

_____

_____

8. I like the slide the best. I've always liked slides.

_____

_____

9. This ride was fun let's do it again tomorrow.

_____

_____

DIRECTIONS: Rewrite each sentence fragment below to make it a sentence.

10. found a hidden staircase in the old house

_____

_____

11. a mysterious note

_____

_____

12. lay behind the creaking door

_____

_____

13. the solution to the mystery

_____

STOP

3A.4

Using Basic Transition Words

DIRECTIONS: Read the paragraphs and answer the questions that follow.

Clue Transition words such as *next, then, however,* and *conversely* help connect ideas within a paragraph or essay.

There are many differences between frogs and toads. Frogs have narrow bodies and ridges down their backs. They have large, round ear membranes and small teeth in their upper jaws. Their long hind legs enable them to take long leaps. Frogs have smooth, moist, soft skin. Most frogs are water-dwellers.

1. If another paragraph were added that told about toads, what would make a good first sentence for that paragraph?

  (A) Their ear membranes are smaller than frogs'.

  (B) In contrast, toads have chubby bodies and ridges on their heads.

  (C) Toads and frogs are similar to each other in many ways.

  (D) However, they lay their eggs in strings rather than clumps.

When I wake up in the morning, I shower and get dressed. Then, I come downstairs and eat breakfast. After I finish eating, I make my lunch. Next, I check my backpack to make sure I have everything I need for school that day.

2. Which of the following sentences would best end this paragraph?

  (F) But I run out the door to meet my friends at the bus stop.

  (G) Later, I run out the door to meet my friends at the bus stop.

  (H) Finally, I run out the door to meet my friends at the bus stop.

  (J) However, I run out the door to meet my friends at the bus stop.

Over the years, Niagara Falls has been a spectacular attraction for sightseers. Observation towers and a special area, Cave of the Winds, behind the falls have allowed remarkable views. At night, the falls are flooded with lights. A steamer, called the *Maid of the Mist,* takes visitors for a ride around the base of the falls.

3. Which of the following would be a good first sentence for a second paragraph?

  (A) One such man, Charles Blondin, crossed the falls on a tightrope in 1859.

  (B) But the edge of the Horseshoe Falls is being worn back at the rate of approximately three feet per year.

  (C) Nevertheless, scientists believe that the falls are approximately 20,000 years old.

  (D) Niagara Falls has also irresistibly drawn daredevils who have wanted to test their courage.

Proofreading

DIRECTIONS: Read each sentence. Choose the sentence that shows correct punctuation and capitalization. If the underlined part is correct, choose "Correct as is."

1. **The last thing I meant to do was <u>annoy the Andersons on arbor day</u>.**

    (A) annoy the andersons on arbor day

    (B) Annoy The Andersons on arbor day

    (C) annoy the Andersons on Arbor Day

    (D) Correct as is

2. **<u>New zealand</u> is home to a playful bird called the kea.**

    (F) New, Zealand

    (G) new zealand

    (H) New Zealand

    (J) Correct as is

DIRECTIONS: Choose the best answer.

3. **Either the garage or the porch must have _____ roof repaired this fall.**

    (A) their

    (B) its

    (C) that

    (D) they're

4. **Neither Julie nor Anna will bring _____ pager to class again.**

    (F) their

    (G) her

    (H) its

    (J) his

DIRECTIONS: Read the passage. Choose the answer that shows the best way to write the underlined section. If the underlined section is correct, choose "Correct as is."

People who live in <u>Nova Scotia Canada</u> **(5)** are called Bluenoses. This <u>isnt</u> **(6)** because of the color of their noses, however. This part of <u>Canada</u> **(7)** once sold large quantities of potatoes called bluenose potatoes. The potatoes got their name because each one had a blue end or <u>"nose."</u> **(8)**

5. (A) Nova Scotia, Canada

    (B) Nova Scotia, Canada,

    (C) Nova Scotia, canada

    (D) Correct as is

6. (F) isnt'

    (G) is'nt

    (H) isn't

    (J) Correct as is

7. (A) canada

    (B) Canada,

    (C) , Canada

    (D) Correct as is

8. (F) "nose.'

    (G) "nose".

    (H) 'nose.'

    (J) Correct as is

STOP

Writing

3A.6

Using Parts of Speech Correctly

DIRECTIONS: Read the passage and answer the questions that follow.

(1) In Great Britain 150 years ago, hospitals for the sick have been unpleasant places. **(2)** The surgeons would be found wearing blood-stained and grime-splattered clothing. **(3)** They often refuse to change clothing or equipment between surgeries. **(4)** Diseases traveled readily under patients in a filthy atmosphere where bedding and clothing went unwashed. **(5)** Hospital food was of meager benefit, sometimes tainted and barely nourishing. **(6)** Them who provided nursing care had little or no training and lacked motivation. **(7)** The wealthy in this period did not send their family members to the hospital but had doctors and nurses come to their homes.

1. In sentence 1, <u>have been</u> is best written—

- Ⓐ were
- Ⓑ was
- Ⓒ are
- Ⓓ As it i0s

2. In sentence 3, <u>refuse</u> is best written—

- Ⓕ refused
- Ⓖ refuses
- Ⓗ refusing
- Ⓙ As it is

3. In sentence 4, <u>under</u> is best written—

- Ⓐ around
- Ⓑ through
- Ⓒ between
- Ⓓ As it is

4. In sentence 6, <u>Them</u> is best written—

- Ⓕ Those
- Ⓖ They
- Ⓗ Themselves
- Ⓙ As it is

DIRECTIONS: Choose the answer that is a complete and correctly written sentence.

5.
- Ⓐ Scientists spends many hours recording the behavior and habits of animals.
- Ⓑ They search for clues to explain why animals act as they do.
- Ⓒ Through careful observation, the behavior of an animal might could be explained.
- Ⓓ Lemmings, however, does an unexplainable thing.

6.
- Ⓕ Glass snakes ain't snakes at all.
- Ⓖ They is one of several kinds of lizards that inhabitate the earth.
- Ⓗ Most legless lizards resemble worms, but the glass snake looks very much like a true snake.
- Ⓙ It can break off his tail as easily as a pieces of glass.

Writing

3A

For pages 83–88

Mini-Test 1

DIRECTIONS: Choose the answer that best combines the underlined sentences.

1. <u>Benjamin caught a fish.</u>
   <u>The fish was large and had green stripes.</u>

   Ⓐ Benjamin caught a fish that had green stripes and was large.

   Ⓑ Benjamin caught a fish that was large or had green stripes.

   Ⓒ The fish was large that Benjamin caught and had green stripes.

   Ⓓ Benjamin caught a large fish that had green stripes.

2. <u>The library had a book on the subject.</u>
   <u>The book was old and dusty.</u>

   Ⓕ The library had an old, dusty book on the subject.

   Ⓖ The book the library had on the subject was old, dusty.

   Ⓗ The old and dusty book, the library had on the subject.

   Ⓙ The library had a book on the subject and was old and dusty.

3. <u>Ju-Yong saw a whale.</u>
   <u>The whale was blue.</u>
   <u>She saw it on her vacation.</u>

   Ⓐ Ju-Yong saw a whale on her vacation that was blue.

   Ⓑ Ju-Yong saw a blue whale on her vacation.

   Ⓒ The blue whale Ju-Yong saw on her vacation.

   Ⓓ On her vacation Ju-Yong saw a whale and it was blue.

DIRECTIONS: Choose the answer that is a complete and correctly written sentence.

4. Ⓕ The fire company responded quick to the call for help.

   Ⓖ My family usually contributes to the fund drive for the fire company.

   Ⓗ They were happily to see the ambulance.

   Ⓙ Nicely people on the ambulance squad.

5. Ⓐ Art class once a week with students in another class.

   Ⓑ Entering a painting in the show.

   Ⓒ Drawing and painting enjoyed by many young people.

   Ⓓ The pot you made is beautiful.

DIRECTIONS: Write a paragraph about your favorite dessert. Use at least one interrogative or exclamatory sentence.

6. _____

   _____

   _____

   _____

   _____

   _____

   _____

   _____

STOP

Writing Standards

Write to Communicate

Goal 3: Write to communicate for a variety of purposes.

Learning Standard 3A *(See page 82.)*

Learning Standard 3B—Students who meet the standard can compose well-organized and coherent writing for specific purposes and audiences.

1. Use prewriting strategies to choose a topic and generate ideas (e.g., webbing, brainstorming, listing, note taking, outlining, drafting, graphic organizers). *(See page 91.)*
2. Establish and maintain a focus. *(See page 92.)*
3. Develop a topic sentence that is supported with details. *(See page 93.)*
4. Organize a coherent structure appropriate to purpose (i.e., narration, exposition, persuasion), audience, and context using paragraphs and transition words. *(See page 94.)*
5. Use appropriate transition words to connect ideas. *(See page 95.)*
6. Elaborate ideas through facts, details, description, reasons, narration. *(See pages 96–97.)*
7. Use adjectives, adverbs, and prepositional phrases to enrich written language. *(See page 98–99.)*
8. Revise and edit (e.g., conference with self, peer, volunteer, teacher). *(See page 100.)*

Learning Standard 3C *(See page 102.)*

Writing

3B.1

Choosing a Topic

DIRECTIONS: Read the paragraph that tells about one student's great experience. Then think about all the good experiences you have ever had to answer each question below.

> My violin competition was one of the best experiences I've ever had. I met people from all over the city. I learned to feel comfortable in front of an audience. I felt good about playing for so many people. When everyone clapped, I felt very proud.

1. **Think about all your good experiences. List the top three.**

   _____

   _____

   _____

2. **For each item you listed in question 1, briefly tell why this experience was so good.**

   _____

   _____

   _____

   _____

   _____

   _____

   _____

3. **Pick one of the items you listed in question 1. Outline the three most important things about that experience that you would want to talk about in an essay.**

   I. _____

   _____

   _____

   _____

   II. _____

   _____

   _____

   _____

   III. _____

   _____

   _____

   _____

STOP

Writing

3B.2

Maintaining a Focus

DIRECTIONS: Read the paragraph. Fill in the circle next to the sentence that does not belong in the paragraph.

 Remember, a paragraph should focus on one idea. The correct answer is the one that does not fit the main topic.

1. (1) In 3000 B.C., the early Egyptian boats were constructed from the *papyrus* plant. (2) With the Egyptian's limited knowledge of navigation, they could only sail with the wind. (3) These reeds, from which early paper was made, could grow to be 20 feet high. (4) The reeds were cut, bundled, and tied together to form the boat.

   (A) Sentence 1

   (B) Sentence 2

   (C) Sentence 3

   (D) Sentence 4

2. (1) In 1567, Francis Drake, John Hawkins, and other English seamen were on a voyage. (2) They hoped to make a profit by selling smuggled goods to some of the Spanish colonies. (3) On their way back from their voyage, they stopped at a Mexican port. (4) By far, Drake is best known as the first Englishman to sail around the world.

   (F) Sentence 1

   (G) Sentence 2

   (H) Sentence 3

   (J) Sentence 4

3. (1) In his book, *Over the Top of the World,* Will Steger relates the travels of his research party across the Arctic Ocean from Siberia to Canada in 1994. (2) With a team of 6 people and 33 dogs, Steger set out by dogsled to complete this daring mission. (3) At other times, they boarded their canoes to cross chilly stretches of water. (4) Along the way, the party would exchange dogsleds for canoe sleds because of the breaking ice packs.

   (A) Sentence 1

   (B) Sentence 2

   (C) Sentence 3

   (D) Sentence 4

4. (1) The "Great Zimbabwe" is one of many stone-walled fortresses built on the Zimbabwean plateau. (2) The Shona spoke a common Bantu language and all were herdsmen and farmers. (3) Researchers believe that the Shona people built this structure over a course of 400 years. (4) More than 18,000 people may have lived in the "Great Zimbabwe."

   (F) Sentence 1

   (G) Sentence 2

   (H) Sentence 3

   (J) Sentence 4

Writing

3B.3

Developing a Topic Sentence

DIRECTIONS: Find the best topic sentence for the paragraph. Fill in the circle next to the sentence.

Clue — A paragraph should be about one idea. The correct answer is the one that fits best with the rest of the paragraph.

1. _____. **Snails produce a liquid on the bottom of their feet. Then they "surf" on the rippling waves of this sticky liquid. Sea stars have slender tube feet with tiny suction cups that help them grip. Dolphins whip their tails up and down to thrust their bodies through the water.**

   (A) Animals eat a variety of foods found in nature

   (B) There are many different animals in the United States

   (C) Animals move about in many unusual ways

   (D) Animals have different kinds of feet

2. _____. **A honeybee collects pollen and nectar from a flower. When the bee goes to the next flower, some of the pollen from the first flower falls onto the second. The second flower uses this pollen to make seeds.**

   (F) It is estimated that honeybees pollinate billions of dollars worth of crops each year

   (G) The most important role of the honeybee is to pollinate plants

   (H) If you are stung by a bee, remove the stinger carefully

   (J) Bees are considered pests

3. _____. **Toads and tree frogs croak in the evenings. Sometimes the chirping of the crickets is so loud that you can't hear the little frogs. But the booming of the big bullfrogs can always be heard. I don't know how Lane Roy sleeps.**

   (A) Crickets are louder than frogs

   (B) Swamps are homes to many different creatures

   (C) Frogs make a variety of sounds

   (D) The swamp behind the house is filled with sound

DIRECTIONS: Find the answer choice that best develops the topic sentence.

4. **Anne Frank was born into a prosperous German family.**

   (F) Her father, Otto, was a businessman. But the Franks were Jews, and when Adolf Hitler took power, Otto moved his family to Amsterdam.

   (G) For two years, Anne and seven other people lived in a secret annex. They had to remain still and quiet during the day.

   (H) When Otto was released from the concentration camp, he returned to Amsterdam. He was the only person in his family who had survived.

   (J) Anne found comfort writing in her diary. She wrote about the cramped space she lived in, about the quarrels and difficulties of life in their hiding place, and about her fears and joys.

STOP

Writing

3B.4

Matching Structure to Purpose

DIRECTIONS: Read the paragraph below about how to plant a seed. Then think of something you know how to do well. Write a paragraph to your classmates that explains how to do it. Keep your audience in mind as you write your paragraph. Use transition words such as *first, next, then, finally,* and *last.* Use details to explain how you learned to do this activity and why you enjoy it.

> I found out how to plant a seed and make it grow. First, I found a spot where the plant would get the right amount of sunlight. Next, I dug a hole, put the seed into the soil, and then covered the seed with soil. Then I watered the seed. After a couple weeks, it began to grow into a beautiful plant.

_____

_____

_____

_____

_____

_____

_____

_____

_____

_____

_____

_____

_____

_____

Name _____ Date _____

Write to Communicate

Using Appropriate Transition Words

DIRECTIONS: The directions below are not very good. They contain information that is not needed. They don't list the materials you need. The steps are not in order, and there are no transition words to help make the order clear. Improve and rewrite the directions.

 Directions should not sound like a story. They should tell the reader what to do.

Once, I was playing with an old sock. I put it on my hand and pretended it was a ghost. All of a sudden, I realized I was using the sock like a puppet. So I decided to make some real sock puppets! I drew faces on the socks with felt-tipped markers. First of course, I had to ask my mother for some old socks to use. I got some thread and cotton and pieces of fabric, and I cut out four pieces in the shape of a rabbit's ears. I got a needle and sewed two of the ear pieces together with a hole at the bottom. I sewed the ear together after I stuffed it with cotton. I did the same thing to make another ear. I sewed the ears on the puppet. I had a good time doing this, and I hope you will, too.

_____

_____

_____

_____

_____

_____

_____

_____

_____

_____

_____

_____

_____

STOP

Elaborating Ideas

Where, Oh Where?

I'm a very forgetful person, so it didn't surprise any of my friends when I shouted, "I've lost my science report!"

Paul, Ansil, and Lena all gave suggestions as to possible locations of the report, but one by one, they were eliminated. I hadn't stopped at my locker, the girls' gym, the computer lab, or the cafeteria. I even called home, after waiting in line to use the pay phone in the main courtyard. Mom was particularly upset, especially since she'd been the one driving me all over town while I was doing research and buying just the right shade of light blue printer paper. She had also done me the huge favor of typing the ten-page report.

"Tara! How could you possibly misplace something so important? Did you check your backpack? Your locker?" Then she basically repeated my friends' suggestions.

Study hall was over. I had one period left before science, and I was pretty nervous. I had wanted to earn another A in science. It would look so great on my report card—straight As across the sheet. But this report was a major part of our final grade in Mrs. Hernandez's class. As I sat in geography, mentally retracing my steps and combing my memory for ideas on the report's location, I had a great idea.

I would simply tell Mrs. Hernandez that I had decided to do further research because I was so excited about the subject and that I hadn't finished typing it. I would tell her that my mother had offered to finish typing it but had broken her finger. I would just have to come up with some incredible and airtight excuse.

As I slowly wandered toward the science lab, silently rehearsing my excuses, I began to feel guilty. Could I actually look my favorite teacher in the eye and lie about my report? How would I feel then? Maybe worse than I felt when I realized that it was missing.

I tossed my backpack over my shoulder, straightened my back, and walked into the room. Taking a deep breath, I knew what I would do—tell the truth.

I walked up to Mrs. Hernandez's desk to speak with her. As she looked up from the thick stack of papers in front of her, she lightly tapped the top report, a report typed on baby blue paper in a transparent folder.

"Oh, Tara!" said Mrs. Hernandez, "I'm always glad when one or two students hand in these larger reports early. I can really take my time reading them then. Your research on whale migration is incredible. Would you mind sharing with the class?"

I thought I would fall over! How in the world had this happened? All this worrying and waiting for nothing!

Name _____ Date _____

DIRECTIONS: Read the story on page 96 and answer the questions.

1. What is the main focus of this passage?

_____

_____

_____

_____

The following sentences are details from the passage. Decide which details help tell about an action and which details are merely descriptions (tell more about a person or thing). Write action (*A*) or description (*D*) on each line.

2. _____ **Tara is a forgetful person.**

3. _____ **Mom drove Tara around town to do research and to buy special printer paper.**

4. _____ **Tara's friends and mother made suggestions on where to find the report.**

5. _____ **Mrs. Hernandez is the science teacher.**

6. _____ **At first, Tara was going to lie about the report.**

7. _____ **Tara decides that telling the truth is best.**

8. _____ **Mrs. Hernandez has a stack of papers on her desk.**

9. _____ **Tara's report is in a transparent folder and is typed on baby blue paper.**

10. _____ **Tara has no idea how the report got to her teacher.**

11. Describe what you would do if you lost a major homework assignment. Use details that tell what you would do (plot) and information about yourself or your teacher.

_____

_____

_____

_____

_____

_____

_____

_____

12. In complete sentences, write your idea of how the report got to Mrs. Hernandez. Be concise in your description of what happened. Do not include any unnecessary details.

_____

_____

_____

_____

_____

_____

_____

_____

_____

_____

_____

_____

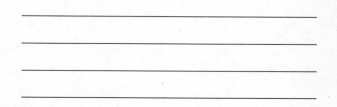

Writing

3B.7

Using Adjectives, Adverbs, and Prepositional Phrases

DIRECTIONS: Underline each prepositional phrase in the sentences below.

1. The watch was still in the box.

2. The children's artwork is displayed at city hall.

3. The cat's food dish is under the bag.

4. Last Friday was the due date for the library book.

5. The singer bowed to the applause of the crowd.

6. Second place went to the girls' volleyball team.

7. My ten-speed bike is first on the list.

8. The baby's bottle was in the dishwasher.

9. The bat cracked in half when he hit the ball over the fence.

10. The prize went to the class with the best attendance.

DIRECTIONS: Add a prepositional phrase to each sentence and rewrite it on the lines provided.

11. Mike called yesterday.

_____

12. Kim searched the garage.

_____

_____

13. Lisa stopped the car.

_____

_____

14. Kira looked puzzled.

_____

_____

15. Peter took his canoe.

_____

_____

16. Ahmed ran the race.

_____

_____

17. The hail pelted the roof.

_____

_____

18. Jordan stopped and laughed.

_____

_____

Name _____ Date _____

DIRECTIONS: Write whether the word in bold type is an adjective or an adverb.

19. **both** puppies _____

20. **blue** sky _____

21. ran **quickly** _____

22. **bad** report _____

23. finish **easily** _____

24. **soft** blanket _____

25. **often** help _____

26. **green** grass _____

27. **large** house _____

28. **black** clouds _____

29. **sweet** oranges _____

30. **sticky** glue _____

31. flew **high** _____

32. swam **yesterday** _____

33. **yellow** daisy _____

34. **broken** dish _____

35. ended **suddenly** _____

36. blew **strongly** _____

DIRECTIONS: Write a paragraph describing your favorite place in the world. Circle each adjective and adverb you use in your description.

37. _____

_____

_____

_____

_____

_____

_____

_____

_____

_____

_____

_____

_____

_____

_____

_____

_____

_____

_____

_____

STOP

Revising and Editing

DIRECTIONS: Rachel has written an article about the Junior Red Cross's clothing drive. The article will appear in the school newspaper. Help Rachel proofread her work using proofreader's marks.

Example:

tom and ben, are going to camping.

they're taking friends.

Lets all get together and help the Junior Red Cross. There are lotss of people needing the organizations help right now. Theyre sponsoring a clothing drive to help people caught inn the recent flood. Womens dresses, mens shirts, and childrens clothing are especially nneeded. If youve outgrown any clothing or have clothing you dont use, please bring it in. Itll help brighten someones day!

DIRECTIONS: Rewrite the article correctly on the lines below.

_____

_____

_____

_____

_____

_____

_____

_____

_____

_____

_____

_____

Writing

3B

For pages 91–100

DIRECTIONS: Read the paragraph. Choose the sentence that does not belong.

1. (1) Niagara Falls, one of the world's biggest waterfalls, is partly in the United States and partly in Canada. (2) My family went there for our vacation last summer. (3) In 1969, scientists did a strange thing at the falls. (4) They shut off the American falls for several months by building a big dam across the river so no water could get to the falls. (5) The scientists wanted to study the rocks underneath the water.

   (A) Sentence 1

   (B) Sentence 2

   (C) Sentence 4

   (D) Sentence 5

DIRECTIONS: Read the paragraph. Choose the sentence that fits best in the blank.

2. One of the nicest things about summer evenings is being able to watch fireflies or try to catch them. _____. Some scientists think the lights are used to scare away birds that might eat the fireflies. Others think the fireflies use their lights to say "Hello" to their future mates.

   (F) My grandma likes to sit on the porch in the evening.

   (G) I usually catch fireflies in a big jar.

   (H) Fireflies need to have lots of air if you catch them and put them in a jar.

   (J) Did you ever wonder why fireflies light up?

DIRECTIONS: Read the paragraph. Choose the best topic sentence for the paragraph.

3. _____. This scientist found out that cars painted pink or any light shade seem to be safer. The light colors are more easily seen. Cars of two or three different colors may be even safer.

   (A) Cars can come in many colors.

   (B) I prefer my cars to be red.

   (C) Scientists studied car accidents to look for ways to prevent them.

   (D) Scientists study natural phenomenon.

DIRECTIONS: Read each sentence. Select the part of the sentence that is a prepositional phrase.

4. The ice cream in the freezer is melting.

   (F) The ice cream

   (G) ice cream in

   (H) in the freezer

   (J) is melting

5. She tossed the ball over the fence.

   (A) She tossed

   (B) the ball over

   (C) over the fence

   (D) tossed the ball

STOP

Writing Standards

Write to Communicate

Goal 3: Write to communicate for a variety of purposes.

Learning Standard 3A *(See page 82.)*

Learning Standard 3B *(See page 90.)*

Learning Standard 3C—Students who meet the standard can communicate ideas in writing to accomplish a variety of purposes.
1. Use appropriate language, detail, and format for a specified audience. *(See page 103.)*
2. Use the characteristics of a well-developed narrative, expository, and persuasive piece. *(See page 104.)*

What it means:
- Narratives are stories or events that have a clear beginning, middle, and end.
- Expository pieces convey information or offer an explanation.

3. Write creatively for a specified purpose and audience (e.g., short story, poetry, directions, song, friendly letter). *(See page 105.)*
4. Use available technology to design, produce, and present compositions and multimedia works.
5. Compose a multi-paragraph piece which presents one position of an issue and provides sufficient support. *(See page 106.)*

Writing Effectively to a Specific Audience

DIRECTIONS: Read each paragraph. Use the paragraphs to answer the questions.

 Think about the request that is being made in each paragraph. Decide who would most likely be able to help fulfill the request.

My family is planning a trip to Chicago, Illinois. We will arrive on July 1, and we plan to stay for five nights. Can you please help us find a hotel? Also, any information you can share about things to do in Chicago would be appreciated.

1. Who would be an appropriate person to send this letter to?

- Ⓐ   the owner of a restaurant
- Ⓑ   the mayor of Chicago
- Ⓒ   a hotel manager
- Ⓓ   a travel agent

2. What needed information is missing from this letter?

- Ⓕ   the number of nights the family will be staying
- Ⓖ   the number of hotel rooms needed
- Ⓗ   where the family is coming from
- Ⓙ   the type of food the family likes to eat

I would like to make dinner reservations at your restaurant for July 3. We would like to be seated by 7:00. Please let me know if you can accommodate us.

3. Who would be an appropriate person to send this letter to?

- Ⓐ   a relative
- Ⓑ   a business owner
- Ⓒ   a restaurant manager
- Ⓓ   a friend

4. What needed information is missing from this letter?

- Ⓕ   the number of people who want to eat at the restaurant
- Ⓖ   the type of food the people like to eat
- Ⓗ   how much money the people plan to spend
- Ⓙ   the name of the hotel where the people are staying

I'm writing a report in school about the state of Illinois. I think some of the stories about our family moving there would make it more interesting. Can you tell me about the time Grandma lived on the farm?

5. Who would be an appropriate person to send this letter to?

- Ⓐ   a business owner
- Ⓑ   a state congressman
- Ⓒ   a travel agent
- Ⓓ   a relative

STOP

Name _____   Date _____

Write to
Communicate

Narrative, Expository, and Persuasive Writing

 Clue   Narratives are stories or events that have a clear beginning, middle, and end. Expository compositions convey information or offer an explanation.

DIRECTIONS: Write a paragraph about the funniest thing that has ever happened to you. Give details that will help the readers feel like they were there, too.

_____
_____
_____
_____
_____
_____

DIRECTIONS: Think of your favorite sport or game. Write a paragraph that explains how to play it. Use transition words such as *first, next, then,* and *last.*

_____
_____
_____
_____
_____
_____

DIRECTIONS: Write a paragraph to persuade your teacher to take your class on an outing to a local amusement park.

_____
_____
_____
_____
_____
_____
_____
_____
_____
_____
_____
_____
_____
_____

 STOP

Writing

| 3C.3 |

Writing Creatively

DIRECTIONS: Think of a good book you've read recently. Use this page to write a friendly letter to your favorite book character. Tell the character why you admire him or her. Describe what you might have done in one of the same situations. Invite the character to do something with you or give him or her some good advice!

Date:

_____

Salutation:

_____

Body of Letter:

_____

_____

_____

_____

_____

_____

_____

_____

_____

_____

Closing:

_____

Your Name:

_____

STOP

Writing

3C.5

Taking a Position

DIRECTIONS: Think of an issue or topic that has more than one side to it or about an issue which you disagree with a friend or family member. Write at least three paragraphs giving your view or position on the issue. Provide plenty of supporting details to back up your opinions and conclude your essay appropriately.

_____

_____

_____

_____

_____

_____

_____

_____

_____

_____

_____

_____

_____

_____

_____

_____

_____

_____

_____

_____

_____

_____

_____

Writing

3C

For pages 103–106

Mini-Test 3

**Write to
Communicate**

DIRECTIONS: Write a paragraph about your favorite way to spend a day. Give details about why these activities are your favorites. Use words that express your feelings.

_____

_____

_____

_____

_____

_____

_____

_____

_____

_____

_____

_____

_____

_____

_____

_____

_____

_____

_____

_____

_____

_____

How Am I Doing?

Mini-Test 1

Page 89

Number Correct

6 answers correct	**Great Job!** Move on to the section test on page 109.
4–5 answers correct	**You're almost there!** But you still need a little practice. Review practice pages 83–88 before moving on to the section test on page 109.
0–3 answers correct	**Oops!** Time to review what you have learned and try again. Review the practice section on pages 83–88. Then retake the test on page 89. Now move on to the section test on page 109.

Mini-Test 2

Page 101

Number Correct

5 answers correct	**Awesome!** Move on to the section test on page 109.
3–4 answers correct	**You're almost there!** But you still need a little practice. Review practice pages 91–100 before moving on to the section test on page 109.
0–2 answers correct	**Oops!** Time to review what you have learned and try again. Review the practice section on pages 91–100. Then retake the test on page 101. Now move on to the section test on page 109.

Mini-Test 3

Page 107

Number Correct

1 answer correct	**Great Job!** Move on to the section test on page 109.
0 answers correct	**Oops!** Time to review what you have learned and try again. Review the practice section on pages 103–106. Then retake the test on page 107. Now move on to the section test on page 109.

Final Writing Test
for pages 83–107

DIRECTIONS: Choose the word or phrase that best completes the sentence.

1. **I saw the _____ tree in the world in California.**
   - (A) tallest
   - (B) most tallest
   - (C) most taller
   - (D) tall

DIRECTIONS: Choose the answer that is a complete and correctly written sentence.

2.
   - (F) He didn't hurt hisself when he bumped his head.
   - (G) Theys have some concerns about the homework.
   - (H) Me and her practiced writing our name backward.
   - (J) Rika and I went in-line skating for three hours yesterday.

DIRECTIONS: For numbers 3–4, read each answer choice. Fill in the circle next to the choice that has an error. If there are no errors, fill in the fourth circle.

3.
   - (A) A more better place
   - (B) to see bats
   - (C) is the Carlsbad Caverns in New Mexico.
   - (D) No mistakes

4.
   - (F) After they finished the books,
   - (G) Tom and Larry
   - (H) wrote the report.
   - (J) No mistakes

DIRECTIONS: Find the underlined part that is the simple subject of the sentence.

5. **The <u>setting</u> of the <u>play</u> <u>was</u> a <u>castle</u>.**
   (A)   (B) (C)   (D)

DIRECTIONS: Find the underlined part that is the simple predicate (verb) of the sentence.

6. **<u>Heather</u> <u>wants</u> <u>herbs</u> in her <u>garden</u>.**
   (F)   (G)   (H)   (J)

DIRECTIONS: Choose the answer that best combines the sentences.

7. **Amanda took us to the pond. She showed us where to find the ducks on the pond.**
   - (A) Amanda showed us where to find the ducks on the pond that she took us to.
   - (B) Amanda took us to the pond and showed us where to find the ducks.
   - (C) Amanda took us to find the ducks, but also where to find the pond.
   - (D) Amanda showed us where to find the pond and also where to find the ducks.

8. **Our town has parks. Our town has beaches. Our town does not have a public swimming pool.**
   - (F) Parks and beaches are in our town, but nowhere is there a public swimming pool.
   - (G) Our town has parks, beaches, but not a public swimming pool.
   - (H) Our town has parks and beaches, but it does not have a public swimming pool.
   - (J) A public swimming pool is not in our town, but it does have parks and beaches.

GO ➡

Name _____ Date _____

DIRECTIONS: Choose the best way of expressing the idea.

9. A The school yearbook needed photographs, so Jason took photographs of his classmates.

   B Jason took photographs of his classmates for the school yearbook.

   C Because of the school yearbook, Jason took photographs of his classmates.

   D Jason took photographs, for the school yearbook, of his classmates.

10. F After we drove to the mountains, we set up our camping gear.

   G We were going camping in the mountains, so after the drive, we set up our gear.

   H To set up our camping gear, we drove to the mountains.

   J Before we set up our camping gear, we drove to the mountains.

DIRECTIONS: Read the paragraph below. Find the best topic sentence for the paragraph.

_____. Since they were so rare, the sight of early motor cars was exciting to the American public.

11. A Today's cars are much more varied, comfortable, and fun to drive.

   B Taking a car trip was quite a challenge in the early days.

   C Not everyone welcomed the first automobiles.

   D Gasoline-powered automobiles were available only to a few wealthy individuals before the early 1900s.

DIRECTIONS: Find the answer choice that best develops the topic sentence.

12. **Benjamin Franklin is one of the most important people in American history.**

   F His influence has remained with us over 200 years. Today, we see his picture on stamps and on the one hundred dollar bill.

   G He died at the age of 84. We still remember him over 200 years later.

   H He owned his own printing business and printed a newspaper. He considered printing his career, but he was involved in many other things too.

   J He was one of 17 children born in a very poor family in Boston, Massachusetts. He did not receive a very good education.

DIRECTIONS: Read the paragraphs below. Find the sentence that does not belong in each paragraph.

(1) Gregory's father worked for the Wildlife Department. (2) One day, he came to Gregory's class carrying a small cage. (3) When Gregory's father left, the students discussed his visit. (4) When he opened the top of the cage, a furry little raccoon popped out.

13. A Sentence 1
   B Sentence 2
   C Sentence 3
   D Sentence 4

(1) In 1567, Francis Drake, John Hawkins, and other English seamen were on a voyage. (2) They hoped to make a profit by selling smuggled goods to some of the Spanish colonies. (3) On their way back from their voyage, they stopped at a Mexican port. (4) By far, Drake is best known as the first Englishman to sail around the world.

14. F Sentence 1
   G Sentence 2
   H Sentence 3
   J Sentence 4

(1) In 3000 B.C., the early Egyptian boats were constructed from the papyrus plant. **(2)** With the Egyptian's limited knowledge of navigation, they could only sail with the wind. **(3)** These reeds, from which early paper was made, could grow to be 20 feet high. **(4)** The reeds were cut, bundled, and tied together to form the boat.

15.
- Ⓐ Sentence 1
- Ⓑ Sentence 2
- Ⓒ Sentence 3
- Ⓓ Sentence 4

DIRECTIONS: Read the paragraph below. Find the sentence that best fits the blank in the paragraph.

The first comic books were made in 1911. But it wasn't until 1933 that they really became popular. The first best-selling comic books were created by two high school students named Jerry Siegel and Joe Schuster. _____. He performed amazing feats.

16.
- Ⓕ Some people are comic book collectors
- Ⓖ They wrote their own science fiction magazine about a superhero
- Ⓗ Nowadays, comic books are created by publishing companies
- Ⓙ Comic books are sold in stores all over the world

DIRECTIONS: Read the story and use it to do numbers 17–19.

(1) Imagine going to a college where you could major in video games! **(2)** Well, all the students at DigiPen School is doing exactly that. **(3)** A man named Claude Comair founded the college in Vancouver, British Columbia. **(4)** It has a goal that is to teach students to create computer animation and to also program video games. **(5)** While this may sound like fun, the school's curriculum is serious business. **(6)** The teachers are professional programmers and engineers. **(7)** The classes are taught year-round for two years of intense study. **(8)** Students typically from 8 A.M. to 9 P.M. Monday through Friday and for much of the day on Saturday.

17. How is sentence 4 best written?
- Ⓐ Its goal is to teach students to create computer animation and program video games.
- Ⓑ For its goal, it aims to teach students to create computer animation and program video games.
- Ⓒ Creating computer animation and programming video games is the goal the school sets for all of its students.
- Ⓓ Teaching creating computer animation and programming video games is it goal.

18. Which sentence is incomplete?
- Ⓕ Sentence 2
- Ⓖ Sentence 4
- Ⓗ Sentence 6
- Ⓙ Sentence 8

19. In sentence 2, is doing is best written—
- Ⓐ are doing
- Ⓑ was doing
- Ⓒ would be doing
- Ⓓ As it is.

STOP

Writing Test
Answer Sheet

1 Ⓐ Ⓑ Ⓒ Ⓓ
2 Ⓕ Ⓖ Ⓗ Ⓙ
3 Ⓐ Ⓑ Ⓒ Ⓓ
4 Ⓕ Ⓖ Ⓗ Ⓙ
5 Ⓐ Ⓑ Ⓒ Ⓓ
6 Ⓕ Ⓖ Ⓗ Ⓙ
7 Ⓐ Ⓑ Ⓒ Ⓓ
8 Ⓕ Ⓖ Ⓗ Ⓙ
9 Ⓐ Ⓑ Ⓒ Ⓓ
10 Ⓕ Ⓖ Ⓗ Ⓙ

11 Ⓐ Ⓑ Ⓒ Ⓓ
12 Ⓕ Ⓖ Ⓗ Ⓙ
13 Ⓐ Ⓑ Ⓒ Ⓓ
14 Ⓕ Ⓖ Ⓗ Ⓙ
15 Ⓐ Ⓑ Ⓒ Ⓓ
16 Ⓕ Ⓖ Ⓗ Ⓙ
17 Ⓐ Ⓑ Ⓒ Ⓓ
18 Ⓕ Ⓖ Ⓗ Ⓙ
19 Ⓐ Ⓑ Ⓒ Ⓓ

Illinois Mathematics
Content Standards

The mathematics section of the state test measures knowledge in five different areas.

Goal 6: Demonstrate and apply a knowledge and sense of numbers, including numeration and operations, patterns, ratios, and proportions.

Goal 7: Estimate, make, and use measurement of objects, quantities, and relationships and determine acceptable levels of accuracy.

Goal 8: Use algebraic and analytical methods to identify and describe patterns and relationships in data, solve problems, and predict results.

Goal 9: Use geometric methods to analyze, categorize, and draw conclusions about points, lines, planes, and space.

Goal 10: Collect, organize, and analyze data using statistical methods; predict results; and interpret certainty using concepts of probability.

Illinois Mathematics
Table of Contents

Mathematics Standards

Number Sense

Goal 6: Demonstrate and apply a knowledge and sense of numbers, including numeration and operations, patterns, ratios, and proportions.

Learning Standard 6A—Students who meet the standard can demonstrate knowledge and use of numbers and their many representations in a broad range of theoretical and practical settings. *(Representations)*

1. Place mixed numbers and decimals on a number line. *(See page 115.)*
2. Show equivalent representations of a number by changing from one form to another form (e.g., standard form to expanded form, fraction to decimal, decimal to percent, improper fraction to mixed number). *(See page 116.)*
3. Differentiate how fractions are used (part of a whole, part of a set, location on a number line, and division of a whole number). *(See page 117.)*
4. Analyze how the size of the whole affects the size of the fraction (e.g., 1/2 of a large pizza is not the same as 1/2 of a small pizza). *(See page 118.)*
5. Describe integers using familiar applications (e.g., a thermometer, above/below sea level). *(See page 119.)*

Learning Standard 6B—Students who meet the standard can investigate, represent, and solve problems using number facts, operations, and their properties, algorithms, and relationships. *(Operations and properties)*

1. Determine whether a number is prime or composite. *(See page 120.)*
2. Identify all the whole number factors of a composite number. *(See page 121.)*
3. Explore and identify properties of square numbers. *(See page 122.)*
4. Compute with 10, 100, 1000, and other powers of 10. *(See page 123.)*
5. Explore and use divisibility rules. *(See page 124.)*
6. Solve number sentences and word problems using addition and subtraction of fractions with unlike denominators. *(See page 125.)*
7. Solve number sentences and word problems using addition and subtraction of decimals. *(See page 126.)*

Learning Standard 6C—Students who meet the standard can compute and estimate using mental mathematics, paper-and-pencil methods, calculators, and computers. *(Choice of method)*

1. Develop and use strategies to estimate computations involving familiar fractions and decimals in situations relevant to student's experience (e.g., If you double a recipe with 3/8 cup sugar, will more than a cup of sugar be needed?). *(See page 127.)*
2. Evaluate estimates to judge their reasonableness and degree of accuracy. *(See page 128.)*
3. Select and use appropriate operation(s) and tool(s) (e.g., mental math, pencil-and-paper, estimation, calculator, computer) to perform calculations on whole numbers, fractions, and decimals according to the context and nature of the computation. *(See pages 129–130.)*
4. Determine and justify whether exact answers or estimates are appropriate. *(See page 131.)*

Learning Standard 6D—Students who meet the standard can solve problems using comparison of quantities, ratios, proportions, and percents.

1. Identify and express ratios using appropriate notation (e.g., a/b, a to b, a:b). Model the concept of percent using manipulatives or drawings. *(See pages 132–133.)*

Mathematics

6A.1

Number Lines

DIRECTIONS: Use this number line for questions 1–5.

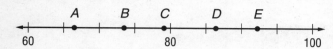

DIRECTIONS: Use this number line for questions 6–10.

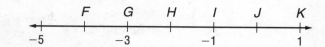

1. Which point on the number line shows 79.1?

- (A) B
- (B) C
- (C) D
- (D) E

2. Which point on the number line shows $\frac{277}{3}$?

- (F) B
- (G) C
- (H) D
- (J) E

3. Which point on the number line shows 66.5?

- (A) A
- (B) B
- (C) C
- (D) D

4. Which point on the number line shows 86.4?

- (F) B
- (G) C
- (H) D
- (J) E

5. Which point on the number line shows $73\frac{1}{2}$?

- (A) A
- (B) B
- (C) C
- (D) D

6. Which point on the number line shows –4?

- (F) F
- (G) G
- (H) H
- (J) I

7. Which point on the number line shows 0?

- (A) H
- (B) I
- (C) J
- (D) K

8. Which point on the number line shows −2?

- (F) F
- (G) G
- (H) H
- (J) I

9. Which point on the number line shows 1?

- (A) H
- (B) I
- (C) J
- (D) K

10. Which point on the number line shows −3?

- (F) F
- (G) G
- (H) H
- (J) I

STOP

Mathematics

Number Sense

6A.2

Equivalent Numbers

DIRECTIONS: Choose the best answer.

Example:

If 87% of the students passed the test, how many passed if there were 100 students?

- (A) 13
- (B) 87
- (C) 100
- (D) 43

Answer: (B)

1. **30 people at the concert left early. There were a total of 100 people there at the beginning of the concert. Which decimal shows how many left early?**
   - (A) 1.00
   - (B) 0.70
   - (C) 0.30
   - (D) 0.00

2. **3,206 is equivalent to**
   - (F) 3,000 + 200 + 6
   - (G) 3,000 + 20 + 6
   - (H) 320 + 6
   - (J) 32 + 06

3. **Which of the following is not equivalent to $\frac{1}{2}$?**
   - (A) 50%
   - (B) 0.5
   - (C) 25%
   - (D) $\frac{5}{10}$

4. **Which of the following is not equivalent to $\frac{3}{4}$?**
   - (F) $\frac{9}{12}$
   - (G) 75%
   - (H) 0.75
   - (J) 0.34

5. **Which of the following fractions is equivalent to 25%?**
   - (A) $\frac{1}{8}$
   - (B) $\frac{1}{4}$
   - (C) $\frac{1}{2}$
   - (D) $\frac{3}{4}$

6. **$\frac{9}{4}$ can also be written as**
   - (F) $9\frac{1}{4}$
   - (G) $4\frac{1}{9}$
   - (H) $2\frac{1}{4}$
   - (J) $\frac{4}{9}$

STOP

Fractions

DIRECTIONS: Choose the best answer.

Example:

Add the missing number to make the fraction equivalent.

$$\frac{1}{2} = \frac{\blacksquare}{4}$$

(A) 1
(B) 2
(C) 3
(D) 4

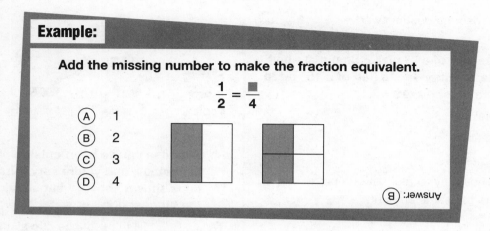

Answer: (B)

1. Add the missing number to make the fraction equivalent.

$$\frac{3}{4} = \frac{6}{\blacksquare}$$

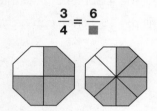

(A) 4
(B) 6
(C) 8
(D) 10

2. Which of these figures shows $\frac{4}{7}$?

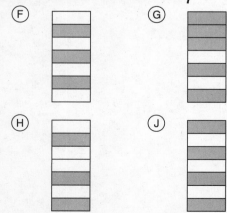

3. Which fraction shows how many of the shapes are shaded?

(A) $\frac{1}{3}$

(B) $\frac{2}{3}$

(C) $\frac{12}{4}$

(D) $\frac{3}{1}$

4. Which fraction represents 4 divided by 5?

(F) $\frac{5}{4}$

(G) $\frac{3}{5}$

(H) $\frac{4}{5}$

(J) $\frac{5}{5}$

STOP

Mathematics

6A.4

Number Sense

Size of the Whole/
Size of the Fraction

DIRECTIONS: Choose the best answer.

1. **Melinda ate half of a 7" pizza; Shane ate half of a 10" pizza; Amanda ate half of a 15" pizza. Who ate the most pizza?**

   (A) Melinda

   (B) Shane

   (C) Amanda

   (D) Since they all ate half of a pizza, they all ate the same amount.

2. **Which of the following represents the greatest amount of money?**

   (F) $\frac{3}{4}$ of a $10 bill

   (G) $\frac{1}{3}$ of a $100 bill

   (H) $\frac{1}{2}$ of a $50 bill

   (J) $\frac{2}{3}$ of a $20 bill

3. **Nicholas read *all* of a 50-page book; Carrie read *half* of a 100-page book; Mario read *two-thirds* of a 300-page book; Mikayla read *three-quarters* of a 200-page book. Who read the *most* number of pages?**

   (A) Nicholas

   (B) Carrie

   (C) Mario

   (D) Mikayla

4 ounces   **8 ounces**   **16 ounces**   **20 ounces**

4. **Suppose you've been outside playing basketball, and you're very thirsty. Using the cups shown above, what should you do to get the biggest drink of water?**

   (F) fill the 8-ounce cup all the way

   (G) fill the 20-ounce cup halfway

   (H) fill the 4-ounce cup all the way

   (J) fill the 16-ounce cup halfway

STOP

118

Name _____   Date _____

Mathematics

6A.5

Describing Integers in Familiar Applications

DIRECTIONS: Choose the correct answer for each problem and mark it.

1. Saturday   Sunday

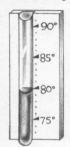 

How did the temperature change between Saturday and Sunday? On Sunday it was

- (A) 5 degrees cooler than Saturday.
- (B) 10 degrees cooler than Saturday.
- (C) 5 degrees warmer than Saturday.
- (D) 10 degrees warmer than Saturday.

2. What temperature does this thermometer show?

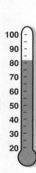

- (F) 87° F
- (G) 82° F
- (H) 80° F
- (J) 78° F

DIRECTIONS: For questions 3–5, use the chart in the right column.

3. Write an integer to represent approximately where the following are located:

_____ porpoise   _____ sea horse

_____ bird   _____ octopus

_____ eel   _____ clouds

_____ flag on sailboat   _____ jellyfish

4. In each pair, circle the item that represents the greater integer.

sea horse, porpoise   clouds, eel

eel, flag   sail of boat,
                           bottom of ocean

buoy, octopus   bird, sea horse

5. Put the following items in order from least to greatest by the integers they represent:

jellyfish, buoy, eel, porpoise, bird, octopus, clouds

_____

_____

Mathematics

Number Sense

6B.1

Identifying Prime and Composite Numbers

DIRECTIONS: Choose the best answer.

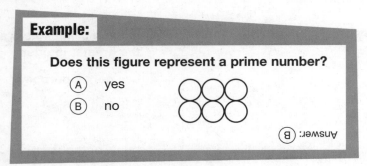

Example:

Does this figure represent a prime number?

Ⓐ   yes
Ⓑ   no

Answer: Ⓑ

---

1. Does this figure represent a prime number?

   Ⓐ   yes
   Ⓑ   no

2. Which factors are <u>not</u> represented by the figure?

   Ⓕ   4 × 5
   Ⓖ   2 × 2 × 5
   Ⓗ   2 × 10
   Ⓙ   3 × 5

3. Does this figure represent a prime number?

   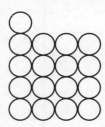

   Ⓐ   yes
   Ⓑ   no

4. Which number is a factor of both of the numbers represented by the figures?

   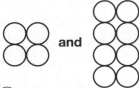 **and**

   Ⓕ   3
   Ⓖ   4
   Ⓗ   5
   Ⓙ   6

5. Does this figure represent a prime number?

   Ⓐ   yes
   Ⓑ   no

6. A prime number has exactly two factors, itself and _____.

   Ⓕ   2
   Ⓖ   4
   Ⓗ   0
   Ⓙ   1

STOP

Mathematics   **Number Sense**

6B.2

Prime Factorizations

DIRECTIONS: Find the prime factorization of each composite number. Write the prime factors in numerical order on the leaves of the factor tree. Check you answers by completing the factor tree.

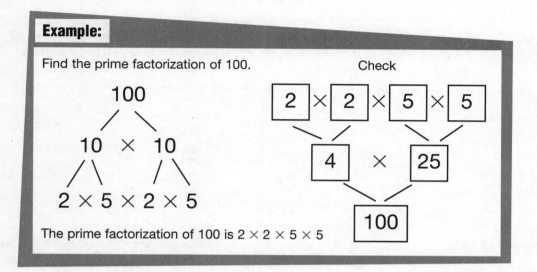

Example:

Find the prime factorization of 100.

100

10 × 10

2 × 5 × 2 × 5

The prime factorization of 100 is 2 × 2 × 5 × 5

Check

2 × 2 × 5 × 5

4 × 25

100

1. 210

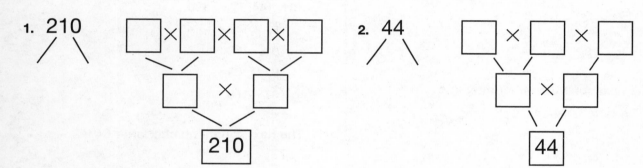

210

Prime Factorization = _____

2. 44

44

Prime Factorization = _____

3. 1,050

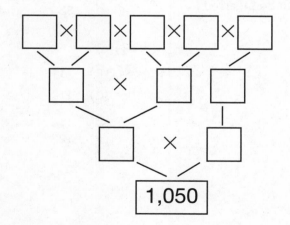

1,050

Prime Factorization = _____

STOP

Name _____   Date _____

6B.3

Square Numbers

DIRECTIONS: Choose the best answer.

Clue

If you multiply a number by itself (for example, 2×2, or 2^2), the result is called a **square number.** If a square number is represented by a grid of dots, those dots should form a square.

1. 5^2 is the same as
    (A) 5×2
    (B) 5×5
    (C) $5 + 2$
    (D) $5 + 5$

2. The square of 10 is
    (F) 10
    (G) 20
    (H) 50
    (J) 100

3. The next square number after 4 is
    (A) 5
    (B) 6
    (C) 8
    (D) 9

4. Which square number needs to be inserted in the blank space?

    16, 25, ____, 49, 64
    (F) 26
    (G) 36
    (H) 40
    (J) 45

5. $9^2 = $ ____
    (A) 81
    (B) 88
    (C) 11
    (D) 18

6. Which square number needs to be inserted in the blank space?

    121, 144, ____, 196
    (F) 167
    (G) 168
    (H) 169
    (J) 170

7. The next square number after 64 is
    (A) 66
    (B) 71
    (C) 81
    (D) 82

8. $11^2 = $ ____
    (F) 111
    (G) 112
    (H) 121
    (J) 122

STOP

Mathematics   **Number Sense**

6B.4   # Powers of 10

Clue

To multiply a whole number by a power of 10, add as many zeros as appear in the power. (*Example:* $25 \times 100 = 2500$)

To multiply a decimal by a power of 10, move the decimal place to the right as many zeros as appear in the power. (*Example:* $8.48 \times 10 = 84.8$)

To divide a whole number by a power of 10, mark off as many decimal places as there are zeros in the power. To mark off a certain number of decimal places, start from the right of the whole number and place a decimal point to the left after that number of digits. If there are not enough digits, add extra zeros. (*Example:* $37 \div 1000 = .037$)

To divide a decimal by a power of 10, move the decimal place left as many zeros as appear in the power. If there are not enough digits, add extra zeros. (*Example:* $92.2 \div 1000 = .0922$)

DIRECTIONS: Multiply each number by 10, 100, and 1000 by adding zeros or moving the decimal point.

	9	45	72.5	.664	.0083
1. × 10	___	___	___	___	___
2. × 100	___	___	___	___	___
3. × 1000	___	___	___	___	___

DIRECTIONS: Divide each number by 10, 100, and 1000 by moving the decimal point or marking off.

	2	7.63	291	18.6	.04
7. ÷ 10	___	___	___	___	___
8. ÷ 100	___	___	___	___	___
9. ÷ 1000	___	___	___	___	___

DIRECTIONS: Fill in the correct answer in the space provided.

If one item costs $19.45, then

4. 10 items will cost _____.

5. 100 items will cost _____.

6. 1000 items will cost _____.

STOP

Mathematics
6B.5

Divisibility Rules

DIRECTIONS: Use the divisibility rules in the table below to choose the best answer.

Dividing by	Rule
2	Every even number is divisible by 2.
3	If the sum of the digits of the number is divisible by 3, then the original number is divisible by 3. (*Example:* For the number 57, add the digits, $5 + 7 = 12$; since 12 is divisible by 3, 57 is divisible by 3.)
4	If the last 2 digits of the number are divisible by 4, then the number is divisible by 4. (*Example:* 132 is divisible by 4 because 32 is divisible by 4.)
6	Any number that is divisible by 2 *and* by 3 is divisible by 6.
9	If the sum of the digits of the number is divisible by 9, then the original number is divisible by 9. (*Example:* For the number 72, add the digits, $7 + 2 = 9$; since 9 is divisible by 9, 72 is divisible by 9.)

1. Which of the following numbers is *not* divisible by 2?

    (A) 46

    (B) 248

    (C) 3453

    (D) 8766

2. Which of the following numbers can be divided by 3 *and* by 10?

    (F) 12

    (G) 25

    (H) 50

    (J) 60

3. The number 216 is divisible by

    (A) 2 and 3

    (B) 4 and 6

    (C) 9

    (D) all of the above

4. Which of the following numbers is divisible by 9?

    (F) 701

    (G) 801

    (H) 901

    (J) 1001

5. What are the first three integers that are divisible by 6?

    (A) 3, 6, and 9

    (B) 6, 9, and 12

    (C) 6, 12, and 18

    (D) 6, 18, and 30

STOP

Mathematics   Number Sense

6B.6 # Adding and Subtracting Fractions

DIRECTIONS: Choose the best answer.

1. $\frac{1}{10} + \frac{4}{5} =$

   (A) $\frac{5}{10}$ (C) $\frac{5}{15}$

   (B) $\frac{9}{10}$ (D) $\frac{4}{10}$

2. $16\frac{2}{7} + 14\frac{1}{3} =$

   (F) $30\frac{3}{10}$ (H) $31\frac{3}{7}$

   (G) $31\frac{1}{21}$ (J) $30\frac{13}{21}$

3. $\frac{2}{3} - \frac{2}{5} =$

   (A) $\frac{4}{15}$ (C) $\frac{4}{5}$

   (B) $\frac{1}{2}$ (D) $\frac{13}{15}$

4. $7\frac{7}{8} - 2\frac{1}{4} =$

   (F) $5\frac{1}{5}$ (H) $5\frac{5}{8}$

   (G) 6 (J) $5\frac{3}{4}$

5. Nicolas painted $\frac{1}{3}$ of a fence. Christopher painted $\frac{1}{4}$ of the fence. How much of the fence did they paint?

   (A) $\frac{2}{7}$

   (B) $\frac{1}{1}$

   (C) $\frac{7}{12}$

   (D) $\frac{1}{7}$

6. Jennifer spent $1\frac{1}{2}$ hours working on Ms. Thomkin's car on Monday. She spent $2\frac{3}{4}$ more hours on Tuesday to finish the tune-up. How many hours in all did she work on Ms. Thomkin's car?

   (F) $3\frac{4}{6}$

   (G) $1\frac{2}{2}$

   (H) 4

   (J) $4\frac{1}{4}$

7. The auto repair shop is $1\frac{3}{10}$ miles from the bank. The bank is $3\frac{3}{5}$ miles from Melodie's home. After she left her car at the shop, Melodie walked to the bank. Then she walked home. How many miles did Melodie walk in all?

   (A) $4\frac{9}{10}$

   (B) $4\frac{6}{15}$

   (C) 5

   (D) $5\frac{1}{2}$

8. A board is 8 feet long. Hank said that this board is $2\frac{1}{2}$ feet too long for the job. How long a board does Hank need?

   (F) $6\frac{1}{2}$ feet

   (G) $5\frac{1}{2}$ feet

   (H) $7\frac{1}{2}$ feet

   (J) $2\frac{1}{2}$ feet

STOP

Name _____ Date _____

Mathematics

6B.7 **Adding and Subtracting Decimals**

DIRECTIONS: Choose the best answer.

 Clue When adding and subtracting decimals, remember to line up the decimal points so that the place values line up.

1. 28.95 + 17.39 =
   (A) 36.64
   (B) 9.56
   (C) 46.25
   (D) 46.34

2. 28.1 − 26.9 =
   (F) 1.2
   (G) 2.2
   (H) 55
   (J) 1.19

3. 0.711 − 0.462 =
   (A) 1.173
   (B) 0.349
   (C) 0.249
   (D) 0.351

4. 56.32 + 2.1 =
   (F) 58.42
   (G) 77.32
   (H) 56.53
   (J) 54.22

5. A book 0.75 inch thick is placed on a book 0.813 inch thick. What is the combined thickness of the books?
   (A) 1.563
   (B) 0.063
   (C) 1.0
   (D) 0.50

6. Yesterday 0.333 inch of rain fell. Today 0.68 inch of rain fell. How much rain fell during the two days?
   (F) 0.347 inch
   (G) 0.50 inch
   (H) 1.013 inch
   (J) 1 inch

7. A rock weighs 0.563 pound. Suppose 0.25 pound is chipped away. How much would the remaining rock weigh?
   (A) 0.313 pound
   (B) 0.813 pound
   (C) 0.538 pound
   (D) 0.588 pound

8. Mr. Anthony and Mr. Androtti completed 0.75 of a job. Mr. Androtti completed 0.222 of the job. What part of the job did Mr. Anthony complete?
   (F) 0.972
   (G) 0.147
   (H) 0.528
   (J) 0.297

STOP

Mathematics

Number Sense

6C.1

Estimating Computations with Fractions

DIRECTIONS: The following ingredients make one batch of blueberry muffins. Use them to estimate answers for questions 1–5.

$\frac{3}{4}$ cup flour   3 tsp baking powder

$\frac{1}{2}$ tsp salt $\frac{1}{4}$ cup margarine

$\frac{1}{2}$ cup sugar   1 egg

$\frac{3}{4}$ cup milk   1 tsp vanilla

1 cup frozen blueberries

1. To make $2\frac{1}{2}$ batches of muffins, about how much flour does she need?
   - (A) a little less than 2 cups
   - (B) a little more than 2 cups
   - (C) about $3\frac{1}{2}$ cups
   - (C) about $4\frac{1}{2}$ cups

2. To make $1\frac{1}{2}$ batches of muffins, how many cups of milk does she need?
   - (F) about $1\frac{1}{2}$ cups
   - (G) a little more than 1 cup
   - (H) not quite 1 cup
   - (J) 1 cup

3. To make $1\frac{1}{2}$ batches of muffins, how many cups of sugar does she need?
   - (A) about $\frac{1}{8}$ cup
   - (B) about $\frac{3}{4}$ cup
   - (C) about $\frac{3}{8}$ cup
   - (D) about $\frac{1}{2}$ cup

4. To make half of the recipe, how much sugar does she need?
   - (F) about $\frac{1}{4}$ cup
   - (G) about $\frac{1}{8}$ cup
   - (H) about $\frac{1}{2}$ cup
   - (J) about $\frac{3}{8}$ cup

5. If Sandra wants to make $2\frac{1}{2}$ batches of muffins, how much sugar does she need?
   - (A) a little more than 1 cup
   - (B) 2 cups
   - (C) about 3 cups
   - (D) about $2\frac{1}{2}$ cups

STOP

Mathematics

6C.2

Evaluating Estimations

DIRECTIONS: Here are some arithmetic problems other students performed. Some of the answers may be incorrect. Use estimation to quickly identify which answers are wrong. Next to each wrong answer, write your best estimate of the correct answer. Then, check your work by calculating the exact answers.

When **estimating,** round the numbers so they are easier to work with. Then, mentally perform the operation to get an approximate solution.

365 × 42	4,773 + 2,531	72,340 ÷ 3,291
≈ 370 × 40	≈ 5,000 + 2,500	≈ 72,000 ÷ 3,000
≈ 14,800	≈ 7,500	≈ 22

1.

    735
 ×   29
  2,131

2.

   45,705
 − 23,369
   22,336

3.

        2184
  35)76,412

4.

    2,413
 ×   620
  149,606

5.

   1,273,412
 +   99,655
   2,373,067

6.

          21
  312)6,552

7.

    473
 ×   684
  1,323,532

8.

    390
 + 7,930
   9,320

STOP

Name _____ Date _____

Number Sense

6C.3

Computations

DIRECTIONS: Choose the correct answer to each problem. Remember to reduce fraction answers to their simplest form. Choose "None of these" if the correct answer is not given.

Examples:

A. $14 \times 7 =$
- (A) 21
- (B) 98
- (C) 7
- (D) None of these

Answer: (B)

B. $\begin{array}{r} 26.16 \\ -\ 8.00 \end{array}$
- (F) 18.16
- (G) 34.16
- (H) 26.08
- (J) None of these

Answer: (F)

Clue Choose the best method to help you perform these computations. Use either mental math, pencil and paper, or a calculator to find your answer.

---

1. $\begin{array}{r} 132 \\ \times\ 4 \end{array}$
- (A) 528
- (B) 136
- (C) 478
- (D) None of these

2. $1\frac{2}{4} - \frac{3}{4}$
- (F) $1\frac{5}{4}$
- (G) $\frac{3}{4}$
- (H) $2\frac{1}{4}$
- (J) None of these

3. $\square + 6 = 44$
- (A) 38
- (B) 50
- (C) 264
- (D) None of these

4. $3\overline{)90}$
- (F) 3
- (G) 180
- (H) 30
- (J) None of these

5. $2 \times 5 \times 9 =$
- (A) 16
- (B) 19
- (C) 91
- (D) None of these

6. $5\overline{)473}$
- (F) 94.3
- (G) 94
- (H) 94 R3
- (J) None of these

7. $\begin{array}{r} \frac{3}{9} \\ +\ \frac{2}{9} \end{array}$
- (A) $\frac{1}{9}$
- (B) $\frac{5}{9}$
- (C) $\frac{6}{9}$
- (D) None of these

8. $12 \times \square = 144$
- (F) 132
- (G) 1,728
- (H) 12
- (J) None of these

GO

9.
$0.12
4.69
+ 5.87

- (A) 10.68
- (B) $10.12
- (C) $10.68
- (D) None of these

10.
245
+ 127

- (F) 372
- (G) 118
- (H) 3.72
- (J) None of these

11. It costs $15.75 per student to take a field trip to the aquarium. If 10 students go on the trip, what is the estimated total cost?
- (A) $255
- (B) $260
- (C) $190
- (D) $160

12. Mrs. Hammersmith's fifth-grade class wants to collect 2,848 pennies for a homeless shelter. There are 32 students in the class. About how many pennies will each student need to collect?
- (F) 50
- (G) 40
- (H) 100
- (J) 75

13. Stacey spent $14.83 at the store. Harry spent $35.32 at the store. Approximately how much more did Harry spend than Stacey?
- (A) $21
- (B) $20
- (C) $50
- (D) $44

14. Golden lion tamarins are an endangered species. Only about 416 still live in the wild. They live in groups of 8. About how many groups still live in the wild if there are 416 golden lion tamarins?
- (F) 50
- (G) 55
- (H) 40
- (J) 35

15. The length of one side of a rectangle is 82 inches. The area of the rectangle is 6,028 inches. What is the approximate length of the other side of the rectangle?
- (A) 75 inches
- (B) 65 inches
- (C) 55 inches
- (D) 45 inches

16. A Tasmanian devil weighs 12,025 grams. A mole weighs about 1/200 of what a Tasmanian devil weighs. About how much does a mole weigh?
- (F) 60 grams
- (G) 600 grams
- (H) 240,000 grams
- (J) 2,400,000 grams

17. Nadia sailed 3.8 hours a day for 5 days. About how many hours did Nadia sail all together?
- (A) 25 hours
- (B) 20 hours
- (C) 18 hours
- (D) 15.5 hours

STOP

Mathematics

| 6C.4 |

Using Estimates

DIRECTIONS: Decide if the answer should be exact or can be estimated. Explain your decision.

1. Jose went to the store for bread and milk. His mother wanted to make sure he had enough money, so she added the costs together. How much should she give him?

   _____

   _____

   _____

2. While Jose was at the store, the clerk added the costs of the bread and milk together and included tax. How much was it?

   _____

   _____

   _____

3. Preparing to carpet a floor, Mr. Mason measured the space. How big was the space?

   _____

   _____

   _____

4. The odometer in a car gives a reading of how far the car has gone. How long was the trip?

   _____

   _____

   _____

5. How much shampoo do you use to wash your hair?

   _____

   _____

6. Tim walked to Amy's house. How long did it take?

   _____

   _____

   _____

7. Lucinda went to the doctor and had her temperature taken. What was her temperature?

   _____

   _____

   _____

8. Robert and his mother need film for their vacation. How much should they buy?

   _____

   _____

   _____

9. Rashawn bought tickets for the movie. How many did he buy?

   _____

   _____

   _____

STOP

Ratios and Percents

DIRECTIONS: Use the table for questions 1–4.

Animal	Number of Students
Sea Lion	6 students
Penguin	14 students
Turtle	11 students
Hammerhead Shark	9 students

1. **Which of the following is not the ratio of students who saw sea lions to those who saw turtles?**

   (A) $\frac{6}{11}$

   (B) 6 to 11

   (C) 6 − 11

   (D) 6:11

2. **What is the ratio of students who saw sea lions to those who saw penguins?**

   (F) 14:6

   (G) 6 to 20

   (H) 14:20

   (J) $\frac{6}{14}$

3. **What is the ratio of students who saw turtles to those who saw penguins?**

   (A) 14 to 11

   (B) $\frac{11}{14}$

   (C) 11 to 25

   (D) 14:25

4. **What is the ratio of students who saw hammerhead sharks to those who saw penguins?**

   (F) 9:14

   (G) 9:43

   (H) 14:9

   (J) 1:2

DIRECTIONS: For questions 5–7, suppose you had 5 apples, 8 oranges, and 2 bananas.

5. **What is the ratio of apples to all the pieces of fruit?**

   (A) $\frac{5}{10}$

   (B) $\frac{1}{5}$

   (C) $\frac{1}{15}$

   (D) $\frac{1}{3}$

6. **What is the ratio of oranges to all the pieces of fruit?**

   (F) 8 to 7

   (G) 8 to 15

   (H) 1 to 2

   (J) 8 to 5

7. **What is the ratio of apples to bananas?**

   (A) 5:2

   (B) $\frac{5}{7}$

   (C) 5 to 8

   (D) $\frac{1}{3}$

GO

Name _____ Date _____

DIRECTIONS: Write the fraction and the equivalent percentage shaded for each drawing.

8.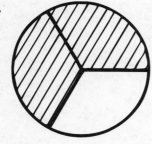

_____

9.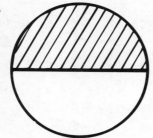

_____

10.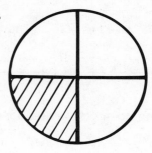

_____

11.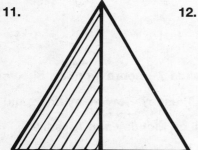

_____

12.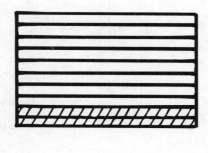

_____

13.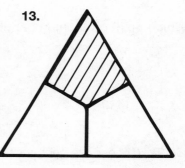

_____

14.

_____

15.

_____

16.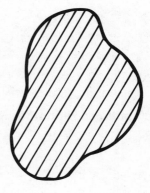

STOP

Name _____   Date _____

Mathematics

6

For pages 116–133

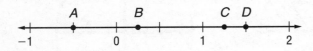

DIRECTIONS: Use this number line for questions 1–2.

A   *B*   *C D*

−1 ——•——+——•——+——•—•——→
         0   1   2

1. **Which point on the number line shows −0.5?**
   Ⓐ A
   Ⓑ B
   Ⓒ C
   Ⓓ D

2. **Which point on the number line shows $1\frac{1}{4}$?**
   Ⓕ A
   Ⓖ B
   Ⓗ C
   Ⓙ D

DIRECTIONS: Choose the best answer.

3. **What number is expressed by (9 × 1,000) + (4 × 100) + (2 × 10) + (3 × 1)?**
   Ⓐ 9,420
   Ⓑ 9,400
   Ⓒ 90,423
   Ⓓ 9,423

4. **Which of these is another way to write 0.25?**
   Ⓕ $\frac{1}{4}$
   Ⓖ $\frac{25}{50}$
   Ⓗ $\frac{4}{25}$
   Ⓙ $\frac{3}{8}$

5. **Write 21 as the product of its prime factors.**
   Ⓐ 32 × 7
   Ⓑ 2 × 1
   Ⓒ 1 × 21
   Ⓓ 3 × 7

6. **48.3 + 6.7 =**
   Ⓕ 115.3
   Ⓖ 54.1
   Ⓗ 55
   Ⓙ 41.6

7. **A wire is $4\frac{7}{12}$ feet long. Suppose $1\frac{1}{12}$ feet of wire is used. How much wire would be left?**
   Ⓐ $3\frac{18}{12}$ feet   Ⓒ 3 feet
   Ⓑ $3\frac{2}{3}$ feet   Ⓓ $3\frac{1}{2}$ feet

8. **Mryia worked $7\frac{1}{4}$ hours Monday. She worked $9\frac{3}{4}$ hours Tuesday. How many hours did she work in all on Monday and Tuesday?**
   Ⓕ 17
   Ⓖ 16
   Ⓗ 20
   Ⓙ $15\frac{3}{4}$

9. **$\frac{3}{4} + \frac{1}{5} =$**
   Ⓐ $\frac{1}{5}$ Ⓒ $\frac{19}{20}$
   Ⓑ $\frac{4}{9}$ Ⓓ $\frac{2}{3}$

10. **Brian made a fruit salad. He included 6 cups of raspberries, 4 cups of grapes, 3 cups of chopped pears, and 1 cup of sliced bananas. What is the ratio of raspberries to bananas?**
   Ⓕ 4 to 6
   Ⓖ 6 to 2
   Ⓗ 1 to 3
   Ⓙ 6 to 1

STOP

134

Mathematics Standards

Estimate, Make, and Use Measurement

Goal 7: Estimate, make, and use measurements of objects, quantities, and relationships and determine acceptable levels of accuracy.

Learning Standard 7A—Students who meet the standard can measure and compare quantities using appropriate units, instruments, and methods. *(Performance and conversion of measurements)*
1. Convert U.S. customary and metric measurements into larger or smaller units. Draw an angle of any given measure using a protractor or angle ruler. *(See pages 136–137.)*

Learning Standard 7B—Students who meet the standard can estimate measurements and determine acceptable levels of accuracy. *(Estimation)*
1. Explain that all measurements are approximations. *(See page 138.)*
2. Describe how precision is affected by choice of units. *(See page 139.)*
3. Estimate the perimeter, area, and/or volume of regular and irregular shapes and objects. *(See pages 140–141.)*

What it means:
- Students should know that perimeter is the distance around a closed figure. Area is the amount of space inside a closed figure. Volume is the amount of space inside a three-dimensional figure.

Learning Standard 7C—Students who meet the standard can select and use appropriate technology, instruments, and formulas to solve problems, interpret results, and communicate findings. *(Progression from selection of appropriate tools and methods to application of measurements to solve problems)*
1. Select appropriate tools to measure, draw, or construct figures. *(See page 142.)*
2. Develop and discuss strategies for determining area and perimeter of irregular shapes. *(See page 143.)*
3. Develop and use formulas to determine the area of squares, rectangles, and right triangles. *(See page 144.)*
4. Read and interpret a scale on a map or a scale drawing using the idea of a constant ratio (e.g., 1" represents 1 mile) and use it to answer questions about actual measurement. *(See page 145.)*
5. Explain the meaning of a measurement answer in context.

Mathematics

7A.1

Measure Angles and Convert Measurements

DIRECTIONS: Use a protractor or angle ruler to help you choose the best answer.

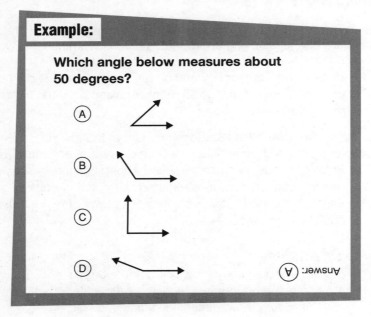

Example:

Which angle below measures about 50 degrees?

Ⓐ

Ⓑ

Ⓒ

Ⓓ

Answer: (A)

---

1. For a class science experiment, Claudia is trying to measure the angle between two streets in her neighborhood. She looks on a city map and using a protractor, determines that the angle must be 82°. Which of the angles below measures 82°?

Ⓐ

Ⓑ

Ⓒ

Ⓓ

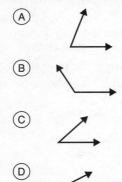

2. Jennifer decided to go for the swinging record at recess. The audience of onlookers stared in amazement as she soared higher and higher on her swing. The roar of the crowd told her that she had achieved her goal. This picture shows Jennifer at her highest point. What is the measure of Jennifer's angle at her highest point to the point on the ground where the judge stands, as shown in the picture?

Ⓕ 101°
Ⓖ 87°
Ⓗ 79°
Ⓙ 73°

GO

Name _____   Date _____

DIRECTIONS: Choose the best answer.

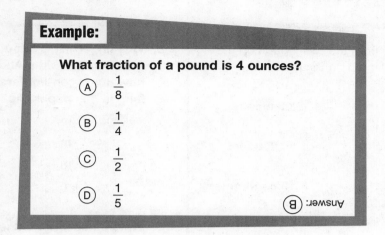

Example:

What fraction of a pound is 4 ounces?

(A) $\frac{1}{8}$

(B) $\frac{1}{4}$

(C) $\frac{1}{2}$

(D) $\frac{1}{5}$

Answer: (B)

3. Anthony's trampoline is about 3 yards across. About how many inches across is his trampoline?

(A) 108 inches

(B) 36 inches

(C) 54 inches

(D) 30 inches

4. How many quarts are in 6 gallons?

(F) 48

(G) 24

(H) 16

(J) 12

5. Phil's van is 1.7 meters tall. About how many millimeters tall is it?

(A) 170

(B) 1,700

(C) 17,000

(D) Not Here

6. 130 inches is _____ .

(F) exactly 10 feet

(G) more than 3 yards

(H) between 9 and 10 feet

(J) less than 3 yards

7. What fraction of 1 week is 12 hours?

(A) $\frac{1}{12}$

(B) $\frac{1}{14}$

(C) $\frac{1}{24}$

(D) $\frac{1}{8}$

8. How many milliliters are equal to 2.81 liters?

(F) 28.10 milliliters

(G) 2810.0 milliliters

(H) 2000.81 milliliters

(J) 0.00281 milliliters

STOP

Mathematics

7B.1

Approximate Measurements

DIRECTIONS: Draw a line from the description on the left to the approximate length on the right.

1. **length of a pen**   **.25 mile**

2. **length of a paper clip**   **20,000 feet**

3. **one lap on a track surrounding a football field**   **13 centimeters**

4. **length of a car**   **1.25 inches**

5. **elevation of the tallest mountain in Alaska**   **4 meters**

DIRECTIONS: Choose the best answer.

6. **A hot dog weighs _____ .**

   Ⓐ a few pounds

   Ⓑ a few ounces

   Ⓒ a few grams

   Ⓓ a few milligrams

7. **Lucinda wants to run in the newly created Fort Worth 10,000. It is a 10,000 meter race. The farthest Lucinda has ever run before is 1/2 that distance. In kilometers, what is the greatest distance Lucinda has ever run before?**

   Ⓕ 5 km

   Ⓖ 10 km

   Ⓗ 50 km

   Ⓙ 1,000 km

8. **This fingernail is about 1 centimeter wide. About how many centimeters long is this paper clip?**

About 1 cm

   Ⓐ 1 cm

   Ⓑ 2 cm

   Ⓒ 3 cm

   Ⓓ 4 cm

9. **Which measurement is about the same as the length of a baseball bat?**

   Ⓕ 1 meter

   Ⓖ 1 kilometer

   Ⓗ 1 centimeter

   Ⓙ 1 millimeter

STOP

Mathematics

7B.2

Choice of Units

DIRECTIONS: Show which metric units would give the most precise measurements of these common items and events by writing the letter of the appropriate units next to each item. Each unit should be used only once.

_____ 1. weight of one apple

_____ 2. short distance races

_____ 3. dose of liquid baby medicine

_____ 4. amount of water in a water tower

_____ 5. distance between cities

_____ 6. height of a book

_____ 7. amount of milk in a jug

_____ 8. towing capacity of a truck

_____ 9. weight of one pill

A. meters

B. kilometers

C. centimeters

D. grams

E. milligrams

F. kilograms

G. liters

H. milliliters

I. kiloliters

DIRECTIONS: Circle the best unit of capacity for measuring the objects and containers below.

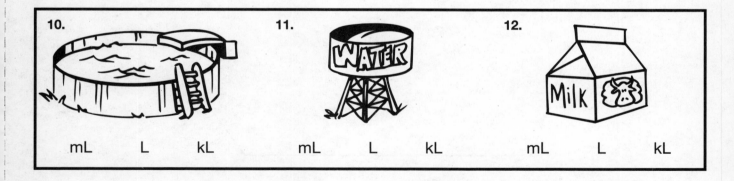

10.

mL   L   kL

11.

mL   L   kL

12.

mL   L   kL

Mathematics

7B.3

Estimating Perimeter and Area

DIRECTIONS: Estimate the length of all of the sides of the shapes below. Then estimate the perimeter.

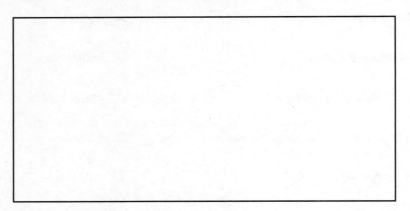

1. **The perimeter of the above shape is about**

   Ⓐ   6 inches

   Ⓑ   8 inches

   Ⓒ   10 inches

   Ⓓ   24 inches

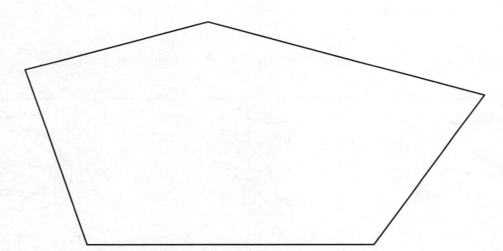

2. **The perimeter of the above shape is about**

   Ⓕ   12 inches

   Ⓖ   18 inches

   Ⓗ   24 inches

   Ⓙ   30 inches

Name _____ Date _____

DIRECTIONS: For each of the following figures, estimate the area of the shaded portion. Circle the number choice that is most likely the area (in square units) beneath each figure.

Example:

You can estimate the area of an irregular shape by looking at the squares around it. In the example to the right, you know that 4 full squares are covered, so the area will be greater than 4 square units. You also know that the total figure is not larger than 16 square units (4 units × 4 units). You can estimate the area of the figure is between 4 and 16 square units.

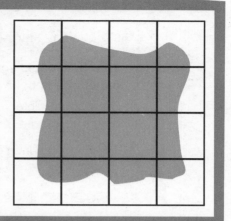

3.

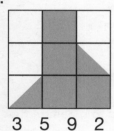

3   5   9   2

4.

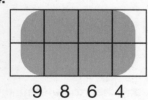

9   8   6   4

5.

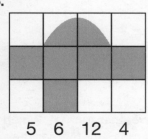

5   6   12   4

6.

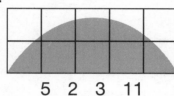

5   2   3   11

7.

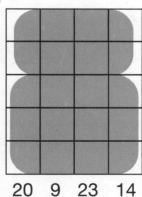

20   9   23   14

8.

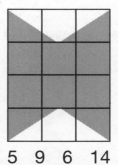

5   9   6   14

STOP

Mathematics

7C.1

Instruments for Measuring

DIRECTIONS: Choose the best answer.

Example:

What tool would you use to measure the length of a pencil?

- Ⓐ calculator
- Ⓑ scale
- Ⓒ measuring cup
- Ⓓ ruler

Answer: Ⓓ

---

1. **Which tool would you use to measure the weight of a dog?**
   - Ⓐ scale
   - Ⓑ ruler
   - Ⓒ clock
   - Ⓓ calendar

2. **Which tool would you use to measure the capacity of a tea pot?**
   - Ⓕ measuring cup
   - Ⓖ liter
   - Ⓗ scale
   - Ⓙ ruler

3. **Which tool would you use to measure the width of a book?**
   - Ⓐ clock
   - Ⓑ calendar
   - Ⓒ scale
   - Ⓓ ruler

4. **Which tool would you use to measure the height of a chalkboard?**
   - Ⓕ measuring cup
   - Ⓖ ruler
   - Ⓗ scale
   - Ⓙ thermometer

5. **Which tool would you use to measure the length of the bus ride for a field trip?**
   - Ⓐ calculator
   - Ⓑ scale
   - Ⓒ clock
   - Ⓓ calendar

6. **Which tool would you use to measure the length of a hummingbird?**
   - Ⓕ ruler
   - Ⓖ scale
   - Ⓗ thermometer
   - Ⓙ protractor

7. **In science class, students had to determine the hours from dusk to dawn. Which tool would you use to measure the number of hours?**
   - Ⓐ calendar
   - Ⓑ clock
   - Ⓒ scale
   - Ⓓ capacity

8. **Phil likes to keep a weather journal. Which tool would he use to measure temperature?**
   - Ⓕ ruler
   - Ⓖ scale
   - Ⓗ thermometer
   - Ⓙ clock

Name _____   Date _____

Perimeter and Area of Irregular Shapes

DIRECTIONS: Choose the best answer.

1. **How would you find the perimeter of this polygon?**

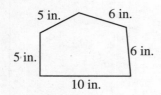

5 in.   6 in.

5 in.   6 in.

10 in.

- Ⓐ multiply the lengths of the 5 sides
- Ⓑ multiply 5 × 10 and 6 × 5 and add
- Ⓒ make it into a rectangle and a triangle and add the lengths of the 7 sides
- Ⓓ add the lengths of the 5 sides

2. **How would you find the area of the polygon shown in question 1?**

- Ⓕ multiply the lengths of the 5 sides
- Ⓖ make it into a rectangle and a triangle, find the areas of those two shapes, then add their areas together
- Ⓗ make it into a rectangle and a triangle and add the lengths of the 7 sides
- Ⓙ add the lengths of the 5 sides

DIRECTIONS: Use the strategy you determined in questions 1 and 2 to find the perimeter and area of each shape.

3.

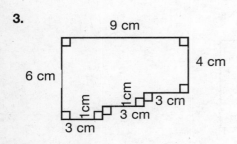

9 cm

6 cm   4 cm

1 cm   1 cm   3 cm

3 cm   3 cm

Perimeter: _____

Area: _____

4.

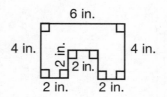

6 in.

4 in.   2 in.   2 in.   4 in.

2 in.   2 in.

Perimeter: _____

Area: _____

5.

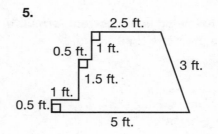

2.5 ft.

0.5 ft.   1 ft.

3 ft.

1.5 ft.

1 ft.

0.5 ft.

0.5 ft.   5 ft.

Perimeter: _____

Area: _____

STOP

Mathematics

7C.3

Area of Squares, Rectangles, and Right Triangles

DIRECTIONS: Use the shapes below to develop the correct formulas.

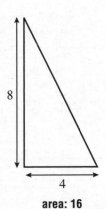

8
4
area: 16

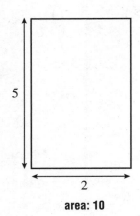

5
2
area: 10

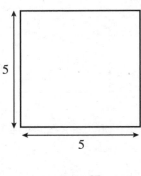

5
5
area: 25

1. **Which of the following is the correct formula for finding the area of a right triangle?**

   (A) base × height

   (B) $\frac{1}{2}$ base × height

   (C) base + height

   (D) $\frac{1}{2}$ base × $\frac{1}{2}$ height

2. **Which of the following is the correct formula for finding the area of a rectangle?**

   (F) (length × 2) + (width × 2)

   (G) length + width

   (H) length × width

   (J) length^2

3. **Which of the following is the correct formula for finding the area of a square?**

   (A) length^2

   (B) 4 × length

   (C) 2 × length

   (D) $\frac{1}{2}$ length × $\frac{1}{2}$ length

DIRECTIONS: Find the area of the following shapes.

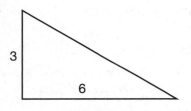

3
6

4. **area _____**

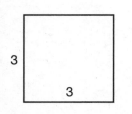

9
1

5. **area _____**

3
3

6. **area _____**

STOP

Mathematics

7C.4

Scale Drawings

DIRECTIONS: Each small square on the grid below represents 4 square feet. Use the following information to mark the grid for track and field games. Label the areas A, B, C, and D. Be sure to leave lanes between the grid areas to give room to walk between events.

A. For the distance run, which goes all around the grid area, reserve 5 lanes that are each four feet wide. Color this area green.

B. Set up a running area on the grid that has four running lanes, each of which is 8 feet wide by 52 yards long. Color this area red.

C. Set up a high jump area that is 12 feet wide and 48 feet long. Color this area blue.

D. Set up a shotput and javelin throwing section that is 32 feet wide by 112 feet long. Color this area yellow.

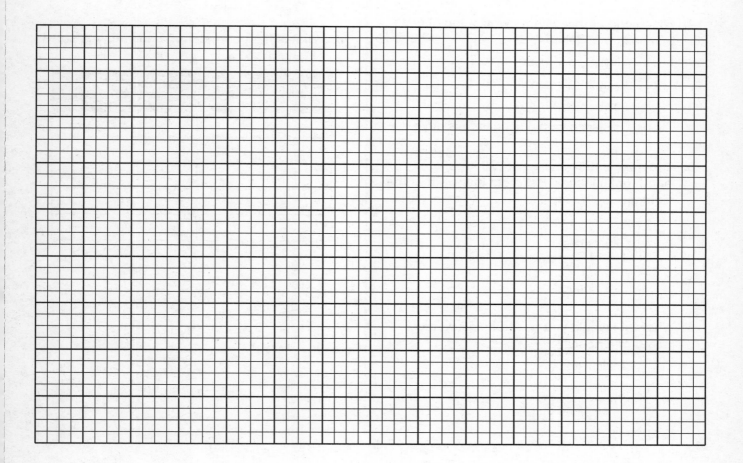

STOP

Mathematics

7

For pages 136–145

Mini-Test 2

Estimate, Make, and Use Measurement

DIRECTIONS: Fill in the blanks with the equivalent measurement.

1. 7 yards = _____ feet

2. 24 inches = _____ feet

3. 1 yard + 4 inches = _____ inches

DIRECTIONS: Choose the best answer.

4. **Which one of these items would you choose to measure in gallons?**

   Ⓐ hamburger meat

   Ⓑ length of a pencil

   Ⓒ milk

   Ⓓ distance from one point to another

5. **A rectangle has an area of 220 in² and a length of 20 inches. Estimate the width of the rectangle.**

   Ⓕ 10 inches

   Ⓖ 20 inches

   Ⓗ 30 inches

   Ⓙ 100 inches

6. **What tool would you use to measure the length of a pencil?**

   Ⓐ calculator

   Ⓑ scale

   Ⓒ measuring cup

   Ⓓ ruler

7. **What is the perimeter of the rectangle?**

   Ⓕ 2 inches

   Ⓖ $3\frac{1}{2}$ inches

   Ⓗ $4\frac{1}{2}$ inches

   Ⓙ 6 inches

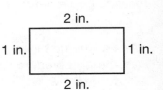

DIRECTIONS: The table shows the perimeters of squares with given side lengths. Use it to find the correct answer.

8. **What is the perimeter of a square with sides of length 2.5?**

Length of Side of Square	Perimeter of Square
1	4
2	8
3	12
4	16
5	20

   Ⓐ 5

   Ⓑ 7.5

   Ⓒ 10

   Ⓓ 12.5

STOP

Mathematics Standards

Use Algebraic and Analytical Methods

Goal 8: Use algebraic and analytical methods to identify and describe patterns and relationships in data, solve problems, and predict results.

Learning Standard 8A—Students who meet the standard can describe numerical relationships using variables and patterns. *(Representations and algebraic manipulations)*

1. Describe, extend, and make generalizations about given geometric and numeric patterns. *(See page 148.)*
2. Describe a pattern with at least two operations, verbally and symbolically, given a table of input/output numbers. *(See page 149.)*
3. Demonstrate equality of two expressions with variables (e.g., 28 + 35 = 35 + n). *(See page 150.)*
4. Describe situations involving inverse relationships (e.g., the more people, the fewer cookies per person). *(See page 151.)*

Learning Standard 8B—Students who meet the standard can interpret and describe numerical relationships using tables, graphs, and symbols. *(Connections of representations including the rate of change)*

1. Model problem situations with objects and equations to draw conclusions. *(See page 152.)*
2. Represent and analyze patterns and functions using words, tables, and graphs. *(See page 153.)*
3. Demonstrate how the change in one quantity affects the other in a functional relationship involving whole numbers and unit fractions. *(See pages 154–155.)*
4. Identify, describe, and compare situations with constant and varying rates of change using words, tables, and graphs (e.g., two quantities that vary together are the length of the side of a square and its area). *(See pages 156–157.)*

Learning Standard 8C—Students who meet the standard can solve problems using systems of numbers and their properties. *(Problem solving, number systems, systems of equations, inequalities, algebraic functions)*

1. Solve problems with whole numbers using order of operations, equality properties, and appropriate field properties. *(See pages 158–159.)*

What it means:

- Students should know the order of operations (parentheses, exponents, multiplication, division, addition, subtraction) and know that expressions in parentheses are performed first. Students should also understand that an equation consists of two sides that must be equal.

Learning Standard 8D—Students who meet the standard can use algebraic concepts and procedures to represent and solve problems. *(Connection of 8A, 8B, and 8C to solve problems)*

1. Create and solve linear equations involving whole numbers using a variety of methods (e.g., guess and check, bean stick counters). *(See page 160.)*

Mathematics

8A.1

Geometric and Numeric Patterns

DIRECTIONS: Draw the next three figures in the pattern.

1.

2.

3.

DIRECTIONS: Write the next three numbers in the pattern.

4. 1, 8, 15, 22, _____, _____, _____

STOP

Mathematics

8A.2

Describing Number Patterns

DIRECTIONS: Complete the table for each function rule given below.

1. Rule: $m = n + 3$

IN(n)	12	14	16	18	20	22
OUT(m)	15	17	19			

2. Rule: $m = 3n$

IN(n)	0	1	2	3	4	5
OUT(m)						

3. Rule: $m = 3n - 3$

IN(n)	2	4	6	8	10	12
OUT(m)						

DIRECTIONS: Find the function rule for each table below.

4.

IN(x)	6	7	9	11	14	16
OUT(y)	10	11	13	15	18	20

Rule: $y = $ _____

5.

IN(x)	1	3	6	8	10	13
OUT(y)	4	12	24	32	40	54

Rule: $y = $ _____

6.

IN(x)	10	13	16	19	22	25
OUT(y)	8	11	14	17	20	23

Rule: $y = $ _____

DIRECTIONS: Complete the table. Write the rule using words.

7.

IN	78	15	41	22	37		55
OUT	65	2	28			3	

Rule: _____

8.

IN	2	9	81	76	37		
OUT	11	18		85		34	51

Rule: _____

9.

IN	82	16	70	34	44		60
OUT	41	8			22	25	

Rule: _____

STOP

Mathematics
8A.3

Variables

Use Algebraic
and Analytical
Methods

DIRECTIONS: Choose the best answer.

Example:

A factory has 314 workers. The owner gave a total
bonus of $612,300. Which number sentence shows
how to find the amount of bonus money each worker
received? Let *b* = amount of bonus money.

   (A)   *b* + 314 = $612,300

   (B)   *b* × 314 = $612,300

   (C)   *b* − 314 = $612,300

   (D)   *b* ÷ 314 = $612,300   Answer: (B)

Clue   Read each question carefully. Look for key words and numbers that will help
you find the answers.

---

1. **What number does *a* equal to make all the
   number sentences shown true?**

   6 × *a* = 12; *a* × 10 = 20; 9 × *a* = 18

   (A)   3

   (B)   4

   (C)   2

   (D)   5

2. **Which statement is true about the value of
   z in the equation: 6,896 ÷ 1,000 = *z*?**

   (F)   *z* is less than 5.

   (G)   *z* is between 5 and 6.

   (H)   *z* is equal to 6.

   (J)   *z* is between 6 and 7.

3. **What is the value of *m* in the equation:
   81 ÷ 9 = (9 ÷ 3) × (9 ÷ *m*)?**

   (A)   81

   (B)   27

   (C)   9

   (D)   3

4. **Which of the following equations does not
   belong to the same family or group as the
   equation: *c* × 9 = 36?**

   (F)   36 ÷ *c* = 9

   (G)   36 ÷ *c* = 6

   (H)   36 ÷ 9 = *c*

   (J)   9 × *c* = 36

5. **Suppose you wanted to double a number
   n and then add 10 to it. Which expression
   would you use?**

   (A)   (*n* × 2) + 10

   (B)   *n* + 2 + 10

   (C)   *n* × 2 × 10

   (D)   (2 × 10) + *n*

6. **What value of *r* makes these number
   sentences true?**

   r + 21 = 30; 63 ÷ 7 = *r*

   (F)   19

   (G)   8

   (H)   11

   (J)   9

STOP

Mathematics
8A.4

Inverse Relationships

DIRECTIONS: Choose the best answer.

 Clue

If $5 + 9 = 14$ is true, then the following are also true:
$14 - 5 = 9$
$14 - 9 = 5$

1. If $a + b = c$, then _____.
   - (A) $c - a = b$
   - (B) $a - c = b$
   - (C) $c + b = a$
   - (D) $a + c = b$

2. If $x - y = z$, then _____.
   - (F) $y - z = x$
   - (G) $y + z = x$
   - (H) $z + x = y$
   - (J) all of the above are true

3. Janie expected 10 people at her party; she baked enough cookies for each person to have three cookies each. However, 15 people actually attended the party. How many cookies did each person get?
   - (A) 1
   - (B) 2
   - (C) 3
   - (D) 4

4. Suppose only 5 people came to the party described in question 3. How many cookies would each person get then?
   - (F) 3
   - (G) 4
   - (H) 5
   - (J) 6

STOP

Mathematics

8B.1

Modeling Problem Situations

DIRECTIONS: Choose the best answer. Mr. Pontario's students are making number charts and labeling the squares from 1 to 100.

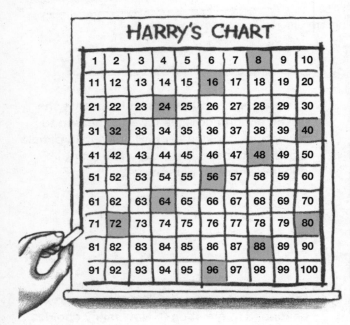

HARRY'S CHART

1. **Liza is making a number chart. If she shades only the multiples of 4, her chart will have _____ .**

   Ⓐ about three-fourths as many shaded numbers as Harry's

   Ⓑ about two-thirds as many shaded numbers as Harry's

   Ⓒ about one-half as many shaded numbers as Harry's

   Ⓓ about twice as many shaded numbers as Harry's

2. **Tenisha just made a number chart on which she shaded all the multiples of 5. Which pattern shows the shading on her number chart?**

   Ⓕ 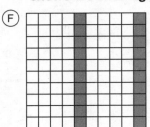 Ⓖ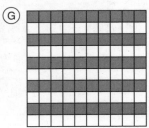

   Ⓗ 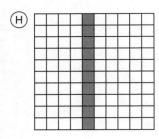 Ⓙ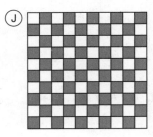

3. **Which of these number sentences would help you find the total number of flags?**

   Ⓐ $5 + 3 = \blacksquare$

   Ⓑ $5 - 3 = \blacksquare$

   Ⓒ $5 \times 3 = \blacksquare$

   Ⓓ $5 \div 3 = \blacksquare$

STOP

Mathematics

8B.2

Representing and Analyzing Patterns

DIRECTIONS: Choose the best answer.

1. **Which of the following rules would give this pattern: 1, 2, 3, 5, 8, 13?**

   (A) Add the previous two numbers to get the next number.

   (B) Subtract by decreasing consecutive integers.

   (C) Add by increasing consecutive integers.

   (D) Add 2 and subtract 1.

	C1	C2	C3	C4	C5
R1	20	40	60	80	100
R2	18	36	54	72	90
R3	15	30	45	60	75
R4	11	22	33	44	55
R5	6	12	18	24	30

2. **Which column has the rule of: Subtract by increasing consecutive integers?**

   (F) C1

   (G) C2

   (H) C3

   (J) C4

3. **Which column has the rule of: Subtract by integers increasing by threes?**

   (A) C1

   (B) C2

   (C) C3

   (D) C4

4. **Which column has the rule of: Subtract by integers increasing by fives?**

   (F) C1

   (G) C2

   (H) C3

   (J) C5

5. **Which column has the rule of: Subtract by integers increasing by twos?**

   (A) C1

   (B) C2

   (C) C3

   (D) C4

6. **What is the rule for the rows?**

   (F) The numbers increase across by a factor of two.

   (G) The numbers increase across by the first number in the row.

   (H) The numbers increase across by a factor of three.

   (J) The numbers increase across by the sum of the first two numbers.

Mathematics | **Use Algebraic and Analytical Methods**

8B.3

Patterns and Change

DIRECTIONS: This is Chris's favorite sugar cookie recipe. Use it to answer questions 1–6.

Sugar Cookies

1/3 cup butter or margarine, softened
1/3 cup shortening
3/4 cup sugar
1 teaspoon baking powder
pinch salt
1 egg
1 teaspoon vanilla
2 cups all-purpose flour

Beat butter and shortening thoroughly. Add sugar, baking powder, and a pinch of salt and mix until well combined. Beat in egg and vanilla and flour.
Cover and chill for at least 1 hour. Split the dough in 1/2 and roll one half at a time. Cut out with cookie cutters.
Bake at 325° on ungreased cookie sheets for about 7 to 8 minutes, until edges are firm and bottoms are lightly browned (don't over cook).
Makes 36 cookies.

---

1. If Chris bakes 36 cookies, how much flour does he need?

(A) 1 cup

(B) $\frac{1}{12}$ cups

(C) 2 cups

(D) 3 cups

2. If Chris bakes 2 batches of cookies, how many cookies will he bake?

(F) 66

(G) 72

(H) 76

(J) 84

3. How much flour will he need to bake the 2 batches of cookies?

(A) 2 cups

(B) $2\frac{1}{2}$ cups

(C) 3 cups

(D) 4 cups

4. Chris needs to bake 3 batches of cookies for a party. How much butter or margarine does he use?

(F) $\frac{1}{3}$ cup

(G) $\frac{2}{3}$ cup

(H) 1 cup

(J) 3 cups

GO

5. Chris's friend Jill would like to bake some of these cookies. Jill only wants to bake 18 cookies. What part of a batch is she making?

(A) $\frac{1}{4}$

(B) $\frac{1}{2}$

(C) 1

(D) 2

6. How much vanilla will she need for the 18 cookies?

(F) $\frac{1}{4}$ teaspoon

(G) $\frac{1}{2}$ teaspoon

(H) $\frac{2}{3}$ teaspoon

(J) 1 teaspoon

DIRECTIONS: Jeff and Mae are planning their backyard garden. Look at their plan below and use it to answer questions 7–12.

1	2	5	9	3	1
2	4	.	6	9	6
5	8	8	6	4	8
7	6	9	3	2	8
1	8	1	0	.	1
9	6	7	4	6	5
1	7	.	8	7	5

7. How many plants will Jeff and Mae need for their garden?

(A) 10

(B) 15

(C) 18

(D) 23

8. Which plants are they planning to use the most?

(F) tulips

(G) pansies

(H) roses

(J) daisies

9. Jeff really likes tulips and wants to plant more. If he takes out all of the roses and plants tulips there instead, how many tulips will there be?

(A) 6

(B) 10

(C) 12

(D) 16

10. If Jeff plants tulips in the whole garden, how many tulips will he need?

(F) 23

(G) 24

(H) 25

(J) 26

11. If Mae takes out the daisies and plants pansies in that spot, how many pansies will she have?

(A) 13

(B) 14

(C) 15

(D) 16

12. If she plants the whole garden in pansies, how many pansies will she need?

(F) 23

(G) 30

(H) 32

(J) 36

STOP

Mathematics

8B.4

Rates of Change

1. **Look for a pattern in the following shapes. Fill in the table.**

Pattern A:

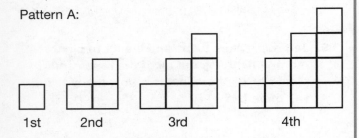

1st   2nd   3rd   4th

Shape	Number of Tiles
1st	1
2nd	3
3rd	6
4th	10
5th	
6th	
7th	
8th	

2. **Explain how the pattern grows.**

_____

_____

_____

_____

_____

3. **If the pattern continues, how many tiles will be in the 10th shape?** _____

4. **Doug is planning a party. He has to plan where to seat people. He can seat one guest on each open end of a table. He must group the tables in rectangles. Look for a pattern and fill in the table below.**

Pattern B:

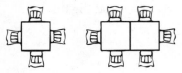

1 table   2 tables

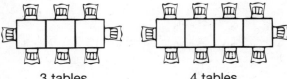

3 tables   4 tables

Number of Tables	1	2	3	4	5	6	7	8
Number of Guests	4	6	8	10				

5. **Explain how the pattern grows.**

_____

_____

_____

_____

_____

6. **If the pattern continues, how many guests will be able to sit at 10 tables?** _____

7. **For pattern A, make a graph showing how the number of tiles increases for each shape. On the coordinate grid below, plot a point for each ordered pair (shape, number of tiles) in your table from problem 1. You may have to estimate the location of the point.**

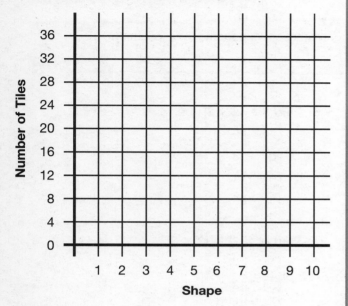

8. **For pattern B, make a graph showing how the number of tiles increases for each shape. Plot a point to represent each ordered pair (number of tables, number of guests) in your table from problem number 4. You may have to estimate the location of the point.**

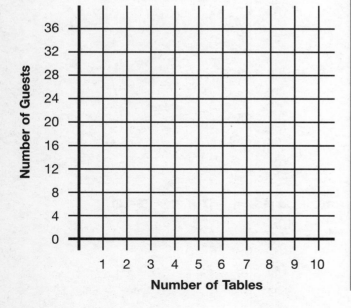

9. **Which pattern has higher values at the beginning? _____ The end? _____**

10. **Look at the tables and the graphs and compare the two patterns. Does one grow faster or slower, or do they grow at the same rate? Write a sentence or two comparing the growth of the two patterns.**

_____

_____

_____

_____

_____

_____

_____

STOP

Mathematics

8C.1

Problem Solving

DIRECTIONS: Choose the best answer.

 Remember the order of operations: parentheses, exponents, multiplication, division, addition, and subtraction.

1. Find 3 + (51 ÷ 3).
- (A) 17
- (B) 20
- (C) 57
- (D) 54

2. Find (2 × 1,000) + (6 × 100) + (9 × 1).
- (F) 2,690
- (G) 2,609
- (H) 269
- (J) 2,069

3. Find (8 × 2) + 4.
- (A) 10
- (B) 14
- (C) 20
- (D) 23

4. Find 3 × (4 + 1).
- (F) 13
- (G) 15
- (H) 9
- (J) 16

5. Find (3 × 4) + 1.
- (A) 13
- (B) 15
- (C) 9
- (D) 16

6. Find 5 + (2 × 3) − 2.
- (F) 19
- (G) 13
- (H) 11
- (J) 9

7. Find (4 × 2) + (3 × 3).
- (A) 17
- (B) 12
- (C) 23
- (D) 60

8. Find 1 + (5 × 4) + 2.
- (F) 26
- (G) 23
- (H) 21
- (J) 60

9. Find 2 × (278 + 3).
- (A) 562
- (B) 281
- (C) 559
- (D) 1,668

10. Find (4 × 4) + (7 × 3) + (8 − 2).
- (F) 27
- (G) 43
- (H) 39
- (J) 37

GO

DIRECTIONS: Choose the best answer.

11. **Wallid and Hayden each have $5. Wallid finds $2. How much does Hayden need so they both have the same amount?**
    - (A) $5
    - (B) $4
    - (C) $3
    - (D) $2

12. **If $c = d$, then $c + 7 = $ ■.**
    - (F) $d + 7$
    - (G) $d + c$
    - (H) $d + 5$
    - (J) $d + 9$

13. **If the first frog took 10 hops and then 2 more, how far would the second frog have to hop to get to the same point?**
    - (A) $5 + 4$
    - (B) $6 + 3$
    - (C) $10 + 2$
    - (D) $9 + 5$

14. **If $a = b$, then $a + 10 = b + $ ■.**
    - (F) a
    - (G) b
    - (H) 10
    - (J) 7

15. **If $c = d$, then $c + 4 = $ ■.**
    - (A) $d + 4$
    - (B) $d + c$
    - (C) 4
    - (D) d

16. **If $a = b$, then $a + 12 = b + $ ■.**
    - (F) 10
    - (G) 12
    - (H) a
    - (J) b

17. **If $c = d$, then $c + 15 = $ ■ $ + 15$.**
    - (A) 15
    - (B) c
    - (C) d
    - (D) 5

18. **If $a = b$, then $a + 3 = $ ■.**
    - (F) $b + 1$
    - (G) $b + a$
    - (H) $b + 3$
    - (J) $b + 5$

STOP

Mathematics

8D.1

Creating and Solving Equations

DIRECTIONS: Choose the best answer.

1. The human heart pumps about 24 liters of blood in 5 minutes. You want to know about how many liters of blood are pumped in 1 minute. Which equation will help you find the answer?

   (A) $24 \div 5 = \blacksquare$

   (B) $24 \times 5 = \blacksquare$

   (C) $24 + 5 = \blacksquare$

   (D) $24 - 5 = \blacksquare$

2. A flea can jump 130 times its own height. If you could do the same thing, and your height is 54 inches, how high could you jump? Which equation would you use?

   (F) $130 + 54 = \blacksquare$

   (G) $130 - 54 = \blacksquare$

   (H) $130 \div 54 = \blacksquare$

   (J) $130 \times 54 = \blacksquare$

3. Mavis works at the hardware store. Her hourly wage is $4.50. How much money is Mavis paid for one week's work? Which piece of information will help you solve this problem?

   (A) The number of hours she works each day.

   (B) The number of days she works each week.

   (C) The number of hours she works each week.

   (D) The address of the hardware store.

4. At the school store, Jose bought 2 pencils for $0.10 each, a notebook for $0.65, and a candy bar for $0.40. To find out how much change he will get, you need to know _____ .

   (F) how much 2 notebooks cost

   (G) how much money he gave the salesperson

   (H) how much he saved by buying one notebook

   (J) how much money he has

5. Joyce collects football cards. She puts them into stacks of 9 cards each. She has 36 stacks of cards. She wants to know how many cards she has in all. Which equation shows how to find the correct answer?

   (A) $36 + 9 = 45$

   (B) $36 \times 9 = 324$

   (C) $36 \div 9 = 4$

   (D) $36 - 9 = 27$

6. Julie is playing a board game. She rolls a 3 on the first die. What must she roll on the second die to move 9 spaces? Which equation will give the correct answer?

   (F) $3 + x = 9$

   (G) $4 + x = 9$

   (H) $5 + x = 9$

   (J) $6 + x = 9$

STOP

Name _____ Date _____

Mini-Test 3

Use Algebraic and Analytical Methods

DIRECTIONS: Choose the best answer.

Shape	1st	2nd	3rd	4th
Number of triangles	2	4	6	

1. What is the pattern for the number of triangles?

(A) The number of triangles increases by three each time.

(B) The number of triangles increases by two each time.

(C) The number of triangles increases by one each time.

(D) The number of triangles increases by four each time.

2. How many triangles will be in the 15th shape?

(F) 15

(G) 20

(H) 30

(J) 35

3. Look for a pattern. Which numbers are missing?

(A) 14, 19

(B) 3, 11

(C) 18, 13

(D) 20, 15

A	B
2	10
5	13
8	16
11	?
?	22

4. Find $(14 + 5) + (9 \times 3) - 1$.

(F) 30

(G) 31

(H) 46

(J) 45

5. If $a = b$, then $a + 2 =$ ___.

(A) a

(B) b

(C) 2

(D) $b + 2$

6. The scoreboard for Kennedy vs. Clark is shown. Which of the following equations would show how many points have been scored by both teams?

Kennedy	33	Clark	24
Time		3:01	
QTR		3	

(F) $33 + 24 = \blacksquare$

(G) $33 - 24 = \blacksquare$

(H) $33 \times 24 = \blacksquare$

(J) Not Here

STOP

Mathematics Standards

Use Geometric Methods

Goal 9: Use geometric methods to analyze, categorize, and draw conclusions about points, lines, planes, and space.

Learning Standard 9A—Students who meet the standard can demonstrate and apply geometric concepts involving points, lines, planes, and space. *(Properties of single figures, coordinate geometry, and constructions)*

1. Identify, compare, and analyze attributes of two- and three-dimensional shapes and develop vocabulary to describe the attributes. *(See page 164.)*
2. Classify two- or three-dimensional shapes according to their properties (e.g., regular and irregular, concave and convex, types of quadrilaterals, pyramids, and prisms). *(See page 165.)*
3. Investigate and describe the results of subdividing and combining shapes. *(See page 166.)*
4. Describe paths using coordinate systems. *(See page 167.)*
5. Determine the distance between points along horizontal and vertical lines of a coordinate system. *(See page 168.)*
6. Identify and justify rotational symmetry in two- and three-dimensional shapes. *(See page 169.)*
7. Identify and describe how geometric figures are used in practical settings (e.g., construction, art, advertising, architecture). *(See page 170.)*
8. Identify, sketch, and build two- and three-dimensional shapes given attribute clues. *(See page 171.)*
9. Copy a line segment or an angle using a straightedge and a compass. *(See page 172.)*
10. Construct a perpendicular bisector of a line segment. *(See page 173.)*

Learning Standard 9B—Students who meet the standard can identify, describe, classify, and compare relationships using points, lines, planes, and solids. *(Connections between and among multiple geometric figures)*

1. Demonstrate congruence of plane figures using transformations (translation, rotation, reflection). *(See page 174.)*

What it means:
- A translation is a move from one place to another.
- A reflection is the production of an image by or as if by a mirror.
- A rotation is the action or process of rotating on or as if on an axis or center.
- Two figures are congruent if they are the same size and shape. They can be mirror images of each other or turned in any direction relative to each other.

2. Determine if two polygons are congruent using measures of angles and sides. *(See page 175.)*
3. Match a front, right side, and top view drawing with a three-dimensional model built with cubes. *(See page 176.)*
4. Identify and describe the five regular polyhedra. *(See page 177.)*

5. Create regular and semi-regular tessellations using pattern blocks, other manipulatives, or technology. *(See page 178.)*

What it means:
- A tessellation is a covering of a plane with congruent copies of the same pattern with no holes and no overlaps, like floor tiles.

Learning Standard 9C—Students who meet the standard can construct convincing arguments and proofs to solve problems. *(Justifications of conjectures and conclusions)*

1. Make and test conjectures about mathematical properties and relationships and develop logical arguments to justify conclusions. *(See page 179.)*
2. Make and test conjectures about the results of subdividing and combining shapes. *(See page 180.)*

Identifying and Analyzing Shapes

DIRECTIONS: Choose the best answer.

Example:

Which of these line segments are parallel?

(A) Two adjacent sides of a triangle

(B) Two adjacent sides of a pentagon

(C) Two opposite sides of a rectangle

(D) Two radii of a circle

Answer: (C)

1. A triangle with one 90 degree angle is always _____ .

   (A) an equilateral triangle

   (B) an acute triangle

   (C) an obtuse triangle

   (D) a right triangle

2. Look at the group of figures. Which figure could be included in this group?

   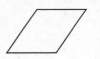

   (F) ⬡

   (G) ▱

   (H) △

   (J) ⬠

3. Which letter is formed with perpendicular lines?

   (A) T

   (B) M

   (C) Z

   (D) V

4. Which of the following sentences is true?

   (F) Only Figures 1 and 2 are congruent.

   (G) Only Figures 2 and 3 are congruent.

   (H) Only Figures 1 and 3 are congruent.

   (J) None of the three shapes are congruent.

5. Which figure has a pair of parallel sides?

   (A) 1

   (B) 2

   (C) 3

   (D) Not Here

STOP

Mathematics

9A.2

Classifying Shapes

DIRECTIONS: Choose the best answer.

1. Which is true about the figure?

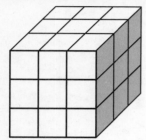

- (A) It has 3 bases.
- (B) All its faces are congruent.
- (C) It is a sphere.
- (D) It has 7 vertices.

2. Which is true about the figure?

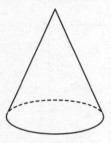

- (F) It has 1 base.
- (G) It is a pyramid.
- (H) It has 2 circular faces.
- (J) It is a parallelogram.

3. Which of these solids has no base?

- (A) square pyramid
- (B) triangular prism
- (C) rectangular prism
- (D) sphere

4. Which solid best describes the shape of a can of soup?

- (F) cylinder
- (G) cone
- (H) sphere
- (J) rectangular prism

5. Which solid best describes a shoe box?

- (A) square pyramid
- (B) cube
- (C) cylinder
- (D) rectangular prism

6. Which shape describes a stop sign?

- (F) pentagon
- (G) trapezoid
- (H) rhombus
- (J) octagon

7. Which is true about a parallelogram?

- (A) It has 5 or more sides.
- (B) Opposite pairs of sides are congruent and parallel.
- (C) Only one pair of sides is parallel.
- (D) It is not a quadrilateral.

8. Which is true about a triangle?

- (F) It has 3 angles.
- (G) All sides are equal.
- (H) It is a quadrilateral.
- (J) The sum of the measures of the angles is 360°.

STOP

Mathematics

9A.3

Subdividing and
Combining Shapes

DIRECTIONS: Choose the best answer.

1. **What will result if the shape below is divided as shown?**

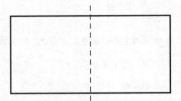

(A) two squares
(B) two trapezoids
(C) two rhombuses
(D) none of the above

2. **What will result if the shape below is divided as shown?**

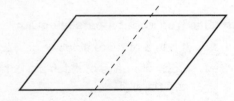

(F) two squares
(G) two trapezoids
(H) two rhombuses
(J) two rectangles

3. **What will result if the shape below is divided as shown?**

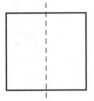

(A) two acute angles
(B) two right angles
(C) two rectangles
(D) two parallelograms

4. **What will result if the two shapes below are combined as shown?**

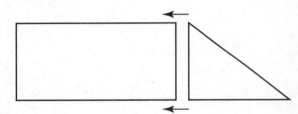

(F) a square
(G) a trapezoid
(H) a rhombus
(J) a rectangle

STOP

Mathematics

9A.4

Describing Paths Using Coordinate Systems

DIRECTIONS: Write the coordinate pairs for each figure plotted.

Clue

Points on a graph are labeled using coordinate pairs. The first value in the pair represents the horizontal distance from zero. A positive number means to move right. A negative number means to move left. The second value in the pair represents the vertical distance from zero. A positive number means to move up. A negative number means to move down.

Look at the example point graphed on the grid below. This point is 5 units to the left of zero and 4 units above zero. Therefore, it would be labeled (−5, 4). The point (−5, 4) is called a **coordinate pair** or an **ordered pair**.

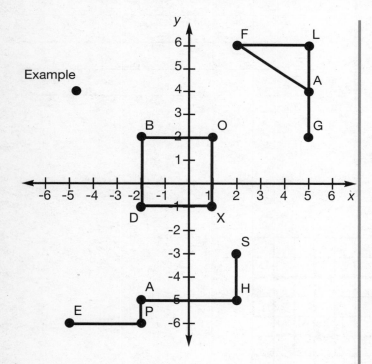

Example

1. FLAG

F = (,   )

L = (,   )

A = (,   )

G = (,   )

2. BOXD

B = (,   )

O = (,   )

X = (,   )

D = (,   )

3. SHAPE

S = (,   )

H = (,   )

A = (,   )

P = (,   )

E = (,   )

DIRECTIONS: Find the best answer.

4. Look at the coordinate grid. Which sequence of ordered pairs would allow you to move from the school to the library?

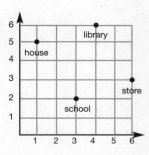

Ⓐ (2,3), (3,3), (4,3), (5,3), (6,3), (6,4)

Ⓑ (3,2), (3,3), (3,4), (3,5), (2,5), (1,5)

Ⓒ (3,2), (3,3), (3,4), (3,5), (3,6), (4,6)

Ⓓ (2,3), (2,4), (2,5), (2,6), (3,6), (4,6)

STOP

Use Geometric Methods

Determining Distances in a Coordinate System

DIRECTIONS: The letters A, B, C, and D are placed in the grid in the very center of town. Each square in the grid represents a square mile. The heavy black lines on the grid represent roads. Use the grid to help you answer the following questions.

1. You travel four miles east, two miles north, two miles east, three miles north, eight miles west, and one mile south, ending at town C. At which town did you start? _____ In order, which towns did you visit along the way? _____

2. Traveling the shortest distance along the roads without retracing your path, what is the distance in miles from town A to town B?

_____

3. Traveling the shortest distance along the roads without retracing your path, what is the distance in miles between town A and town D?

_____

4. Describe the longest route, along the roads, to get from town A to town D.

_____

_____

_____

_____

5. Describe the shortest route, along the roads, to get from town B to town C.

_____

_____

_____

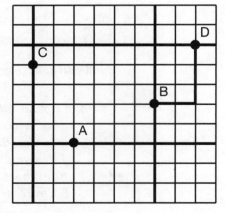

Mathematics

Rotational Symmetry

DIRECTIONS: Write *yes* beneath each object that has rotational symmetry and *no* beneath objects that do not have rotational symmetry.

Clue

To check if an object has rotational symmetry, follow these steps.
- Trace the object using a small square of tracing paper.
- Place the traced image on top of the original image. Hold the traced image by a pencil-point in the center of the image.
- Rotate your tracing paper around the center point. If the traced image matches exactly with the original image before you have rotated the paper in one full circle, then the shape has rotational symmetry.

1.

_____

2.

_____

3.

_____

4.

_____

5.

_____

6.

_____

7.

_____

8.

_____

9.

_____

10.

_____

11.

_____

12.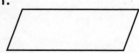

_____

STOP

Mathematics

9A.7

Geometric Figures in Everyday Life

DIRECTIONS: For each geometric figure listed, give at least two examples that you find in your environment. For example, a window in your living room might be a rectangle.

1. **Square**

_____

_____

2. **Rectangle**

_____

_____

3. **Circle**

_____

_____

4. **Cone**

_____

_____

5. **Cylinder**

_____

_____

6. **Sphere**

_____

_____

STOP

Mathematics

9A.8

Sketching Shapes

DIRECTIONS: Name and draw the described polygon.

Clue Before you choose an answer, ask yourself if the answer makes sense. If you are confused by a problem, read it again. If you are still confused, skip the problem and come back to it later.

1. **Polygon with three equal sides.**

   Shape: _____

2. **Polygon with opposite sides equal and four right angles.**

   Shape: _____

3. **Polygon with three sides of different lengths.**

   Shape: _____

4. **Polygon with four sides equal, opposite sides parallel, and opposite angles equal.**

   Shape: _____

5. **A three-dimensional shape with a polygon for a base and triangles with a common vertex.**

   Shape: _____

6. **Completely curved three-dimensional shape.**

   Shape: _____

STOP

Mathematics

9A.9

Copying a Line Segment

DIRECTIONS: Copy the following line segments on the reference lines provided.

Clue

To copy a line segment:
1. Place a starting point on the reference line.
2. Place the point of the compass on point A.
3. Stretch the compass so that the pencil is exactly on B.
4. Without changing the span of the compass, place the compass point on the starting point on the reference line and swing the pencil so that it crosses the reference line. Label your copy.

1.

A ——————————————————————— B

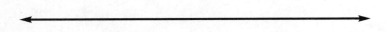

2.

A ——————————————————————— B

3.

A ————————————— B

4.

A ————————————————————————————— B

STOP

Mathematics

9A.10

Perpendicular Bisector
of a Line Segment

DIRECTIONS: Construct perpendicular bisectors of the following line segments.

Given a line segment AB

A ————————————— B

open your compass more than half of the distance between A and B, and scribe arcs of the same radius centered at A and B.

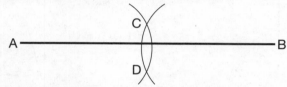

Call the two points where these two arcs meet C and D. Draw the line between C and D.

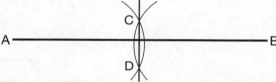

CD is the perpendicular bisector of the line segment AB. Call the point where CD intersects AB E.

1.

G ————————————————————— H

2.

L ——————————— M

3.

O ————————————————— R

STOP

DIRECTIONS: Choose the best answer.

1. **Which pair of shapes is congruent?**

   Ⓐ

   Ⓑ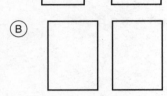

   Ⓒ

   Ⓓ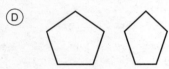

2. **Which line segment seems to be congruent to $\overline{XY}$?**

   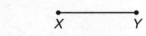

   Ⓕ

   Ⓖ

   Ⓗ

   Ⓙ

3. **Which pair of shapes is congruent?**

   Ⓐ

   Ⓑ

   Ⓒ

   Ⓓ

4. **Which line segment seems to be congruent to $\overline{AB}$?**

   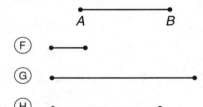

5. **Which pair of shapes is congruent?**

   Ⓐ

   Ⓑ

   Ⓒ

   Ⓓ

STOP

Mathematics

9B.2 **Similar and Congruent Figures**

DIRECTIONS: Measure the angles and sides of the shapes. Write *congruent* or *similar* below each set of shapes based on your findings.

Congruent shapes have the same measures of angles and sides.
Similar shapes have the same measures of angles, but not of sides.

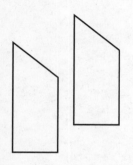

1. _____

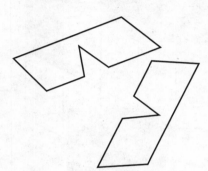

2. _____

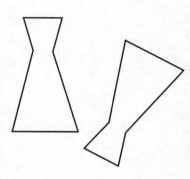

3. _____

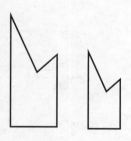

4. _____

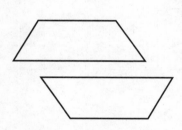

5. _____

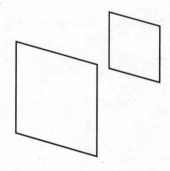

6. _____

7. _____

STOP

Mathematics

9B.3

Matching Views of
Three-Dimensional Models

DIRECTIONS: Choose the best answer.

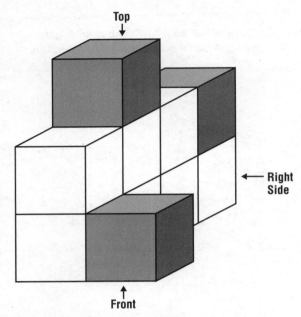

1. Which of these shows the right side view of the figure above?

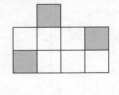   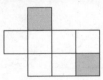   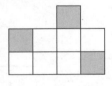   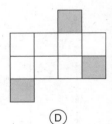

Ⓐ   Ⓑ   Ⓒ   Ⓓ

2. Which of these shows the front view of the figure above?

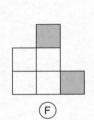   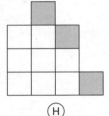   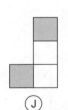

Ⓕ   Ⓖ   Ⓗ   Ⓙ

3. Which of these shows the top view of the figure above?

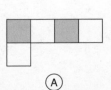   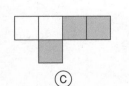   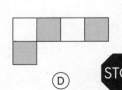

Ⓐ   Ⓑ   Ⓒ   Ⓓ

STOP

Mathematics

9B.4

Regular Polyhedra

DIRECTIONS: Use the table below to answer the following questions.

Polyhedron	Number of Faces	Shape of Faces
Tetrahedron	4	Equilateral Triangle (3-sided)
Cube (Hexahedron)	6	Square (4-sided)
Octahedron	8	Equilateral Triangle (3-sided)
Dodecahedron	12	Pentagon (5-sided)
Icosahedron	20	Equilateral Triangle (3-sided)

Clue A **polyhedron** is a three-dimensional solid made from flat sides, or faces. The faces of the five **regular polyhedron** are all regular polygons (a polygon with sides of equal length placed symmetrically around a common center).

1. **Which figure is not a regular polyhedron?**

   1   2   3   4

(A) 1
(B) 2
(C) 3
(D) 4

2. **Which polygon is on the face of a dodecahedron?**

(F) pentagon
(G) square
(H) octagon
(J) equilateral triangle

3. **A polyhedron whose faces are rectangular is not a regular polyhedron because _____.**

(A) a rectangle has too many sides
(B) a rectangle does not have enough sides
(C) the sides of a rectangle are not of equal length
(D) the sides of a rectangle are of equal length

4. **Identify the figure below.**

(F) hexahedron
(G) dodecahedron
(H) octahedron
(J) icosahedron

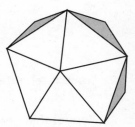

177

Name _____   Date _____

Mathematics

Tessellations

DIRECTIONS: Follow these steps to make a tessellation.

1. **Begin your incision/cut at a vertex (corner) on the shape and cut any way you want to as long as you exit from the adjacent vertex.**

   (A) In this figure, the cut was started at the vertex on the top left corner and ended at the vertex on the top right corner. These are *adjacent* vertices.

   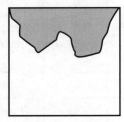

   (B) Slide out the piece that you have cut. Do not flip it over or rotate it.

   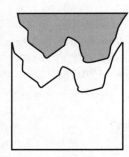

   (C) Slide the part to the opposite side and secure it there with tape. Be careful not to overlap the piece or make a gap. It should fit perfectly at the seam. This is your tessellating tile.

   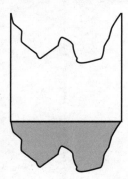

2. **Trace it repeatedly without flipping, rotating, or leaving gaps and making overlaps.**

3. **Repeat this until you fill up the page. Do not worry about shapes that are cut off by your paper's edge; remember a tessellation can go on forever on a continuous plane.**

4. **Make your own tessellation that is different from this example.**

STOP

Mathematics

9C.1

Testing Conjectures About Mathematical Properties

DIRECTIONS: Answer the following questions.

1. **Without measuring, tell the measurement of the missing angle below. Then write a brief argument to justify your answer.**

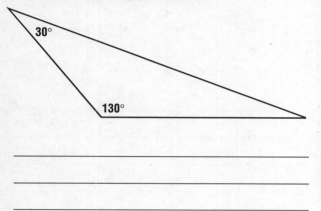

_____

_____

_____

_____

_____

2. **Without measuring, tell the measurement of the missing angle below. Then write a brief argument to justify your answer.**

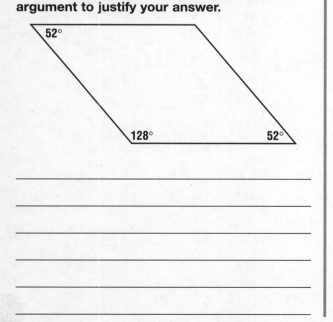

_____

_____

_____

_____

3. **If shape A were cut out and folded to make a three-dimensional figure, tell what type of figure it would be and explain your answer.**

Shape A

_____

_____

_____

_____

_____

_____

_____

STOP

Mathematics

| 9C.2 |

Testing Conjectures About Subdividing Shapes

DIRECTIONS: Answer the following questions.

1. Explain what will result if the shape below is divided as shown. Use angle and side measurements of the shapes to justify your answer.

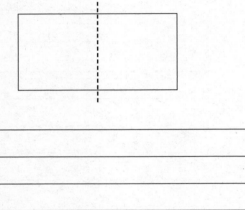

_____

_____

_____

_____

_____

2. Explain what will result if the shape below is divided as shown. Use angle and side measurements of the shapes to justify your answer.

_____

_____

_____

_____

_____

_____

STOP

Mathematics

9

For pages 164–180

Use Geometric
Methods

DIRECTIONS: Choose the best answer.

1. Which of the figures below is a sphere?

2. How many faces does a cube have?

- (F) 5
- (G) 6
- (H) 7
- (J) 8

3. Which shape contains the most angles?

- (A) a quadrilateral
- (B) a hexagon
- (C) a pentagon
- (D) an octagon

4. Which of these shows the top view of the figure below?

(F)   (G)   (H)   (J)

DIRECTIONS: Use this graph to answer questions 5–7.

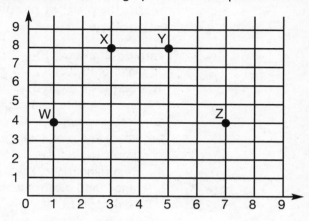

5. What point is at (5,8)?

- (A) W
- (B) X
- (C) Y
- (D) Z

6. How would you have to move to go from point W to point X?

- (F) −2 units horizontally, +4 units vertically
- (G) −2 units horizontally, −4 units vertically
- (H) +2 units horizontally, −4 units vertically
- (J) +2 units horizontally, +4 units vertically

7. If you connected points W and X, points X and Y, points Y and Z, and points Z and W, what shape would you have?

- (A) a rhombus
- (B) a trapezoid
- (C) a hexagon
- (D) a pentagon

STOP

Mathematics Standards

Collect, Organize, and Analyze Data

Goal 10: Collect, organize, and analyze data using statistical methods; predict results; and interpret certainty using concepts of probability.

Learning Standard 10A—Students who meet the standard can organize, describe, and make predictions from existing data. *(Data analysis)*
1. Represent given data using double bar graphs, double line graphs, and stem and leaf plots with and without technology. *(See pages 183–184.)*
2. Select an appropriate graph format to display given data. *(See page 185.)*
3. Read, interpret, infer, predict, draw conclusions, and evaluate data from any graph. *(See page 186.)*
4. Determine mean, median, mode, minimum value, maximum value, and range, and discuss what each does to help interpret a given set of data. *(See page 187.)*

What it means:
Students should know that the
- range of a set of data is the difference between the greatest value and the lowest value of the set.
- mean of a set of data is the sum of the data divided by the number of pieces of data (average).
- median of a set of data is the number in the middle when the numbers are put in order.
- mode of a set of data is the one that occurs most often.

Learning Standard 10B—Students who meet the standard can formulate questions, design data collection methods, gather and analyze data, and communicate findings. *(Data Collection)*
1. Design investigations to address a question and consider how data-collection methods affect the nature of a data set. *(See page 188.)*
2. Propose and justify conclusions and predictions that are based on data and design studies to further investigate the conclusions or predictions. *(See page 189.)*

Learning Standard 10C—Students who meet the standard can determine, describe, and apply the probabilities of events. *(Probability including counting techniques)*
1. List all possible outcomes of compound, independent events (e.g., toss a coin and spin a spinner). *(See page 190.)*
2. Assign a value of zero to probabilities that are impossible and a value of one to probabilities that are certain. *(See page 191.)*
3. Express simple probabilities as a fraction between zero and one. *(See page 192.)*
4. Predict the probability of outcomes of simple experiments and test the predictions. *(See page 193.)*

Mathematics
10A.1

Collect, Organize, and
Analyze Data

Double Bar Graphs, Double Line Graphs, and Stem-and-Leaf Plots

DIRECTIONS: Represent the data in the following questions as directed.

In a stem-and-leaf plot, each data value is divided into a **"stem"** and a **"leaf."**
The last digit of the number is usually the leaf; the digits to the left of the leaf
form the stem. The number 456 would be split as:

stem   45
leaf   6

1. The school drama club hopes to raise enough money to buy costumes for their first play. Each of the 10 members was given 15 tins of popcorn and 15 bags of pretzels to sell. The table lists the number of items each member sold. Construct a double bar graph in the space below, or on graph paper, to show the results of the sale.

Member	Popcorn	Pretzels
Amelia	6	12
Bobby	10	12
Carla	14	9
Daniel	15	14
Beth	13	4
Frank	7	15
Gerry	7	5
Hank	12	10
Isabella	1	13
Jim	11	11

GO

2. **The table lists the number of rainy days per month in a city in Texas for two consecutive years. Construct a double line graph in the space below to show the data.**

Month	2003	2004
January	8	6
February	5	8
March	8	5
April	8	8
May	10	13
June	13	9
July	17	8
August	17	15
September	25	19
October	20	18
November	7	8
December	9	9

3. **A math teacher has just finished grading the tests for the 15 students in her class. The test scores out of 40 points are: 25, 26, 28, 30, 32, 32, 34, 35, 35, 37, 38, 39, 40, 40, 40. Construct a stem-and-leaf plot for the data. The first one has been done for you.**

Test Scores (out of 40 pts)	
Stem	Leaf
2	5

Legend: 2 | 5 means 25

Mathematics

| 10A.2 |

Displaying Data

DIRECTIONS: The same data can be represented different ways depending on which style of chart is used. Use the information in the following table to fill in the bar graph and circle chart below.

School Election Results			
Grade	Votes for Blue Party	Votes for Red Party	Total Votes by Grade
Third	25	5	30
Fourth	10	16	26
Fifth	15	21	36
Total Votes by Party	50	42	

School Election Results

1.

Number of Votes (y-axis: 60, 50, 40, 30, 20, 10)

Grade	
☐	= Red Party
▨	= Blue Party

Voters in Each Grade

2.

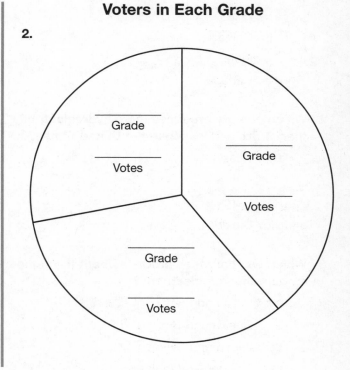

Grade _____
Votes _____

Grade _____
Votes _____

Grade _____
Votes _____

STOP

Name ______________________________ Date ______________

Mathematics

10A.3

Analyzing Data

Collect, Organize, and Analyze Data

DIRECTIONS: Use the graph below for questions 1–3.

Top Countries Generating Hydroelectric Power

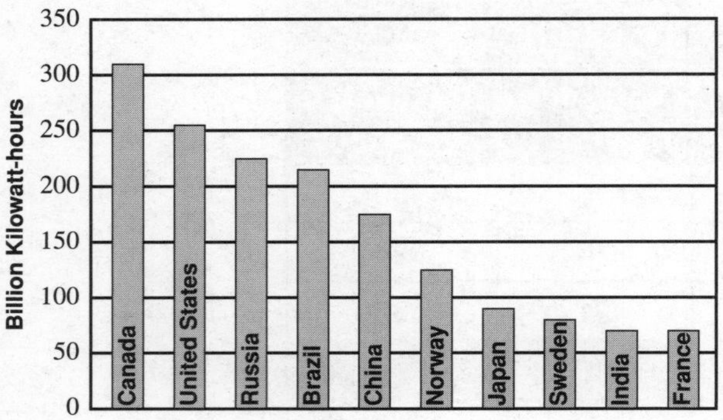

1. Which country produces the most hydroelectricity?

Ⓐ Brazil
Ⓑ China
Ⓒ India
Ⓓ Canada

2. Which country produces more hydroelectricity than Brazil and less than the United States?

Ⓕ Russia
Ⓖ China
Ⓗ Canada
Ⓙ Brazil

3. Which two countries produce about the same amount of hydroelectricity?

Ⓐ India and France
Ⓑ Russia and Brazil
Ⓒ Japan and Sweden
Ⓓ Sweden and India

DIRECTIONS: Use the graph below for questions 4–6.

Number of Students at Highview School

Grade Level	Number of Students
Kindergarten	🧍🧍🧍🧍🧍🧍🧍🧍🧍
1st Grade	🧍🧍🧍🧍🧍🧍🧍🧍🧍🧍🧍🧍
2nd Grade	🧍🧍🧍🧍🧍🧍🧍
3rd Grade	🧍🧍🧍🧍🧍🧍🧍🧍
4th Grade	🧍🧍🧍🧍🧍🧍🧍🧍🧍🧍🧍🧍
5th Grade	🧍🧍🧍🧍🧍🧍🧍

Key: 🧍 = 5 students

4. How many students attend Highview School?

Ⓕ 275
Ⓖ 290
Ⓗ 315
Ⓙ 192

5. How many Highview students are fourth graders?

Ⓐ 30
Ⓑ 40
Ⓒ 50
Ⓓ 60

6. What is the mean or average number of students in each grade at Highview? (round to the nearest one)

Ⓕ 41
Ⓖ 46
Ⓗ 38
Ⓙ 52

STOP

Mathematics

10A.4

Mean, Median, Mode, and Range

Collect, Organize, and
Analyze Data

DIRECTIONS: For each store, calculate the mean, median, mode, and range of prices for soccer cleats. Also determine the minimum value and maximum value of soccer cleats at each store. All prices have been rounded to the nearest dollar.

1. **Store 1 Prices**

$45 $32
$45 $70 $45
$20 $48 $55
$50 $32

Mean: _____

Median: _____

Mode: _____

Range: _____

Minimum Value: _____

Maximum Value: _____

2. **Store 2 Prices**

$35 $40
$35 $25 $75
$50 $63 $80
$42 $35

Mean: _____

Median: _____

Mode: _____

Range: _____

Minimum Value: _____

Maximum Value: _____

3. **Store 3 Prices**

$85 $50 $45
$60 $45 $80
$85 $20 $85
$50 $100

Mean: _____

Median: _____

Mode: _____

Range: _____

Minimum Value: _____

Maximum Value: _____

4. **Store 4 Prices**

$55 $60
$88 $60 $32
$80 $48 $64
$80 $60

Mean: _____

Median: _____

Mode: _____

Range: _____

Minimum Value: _____

Maximum Value: _____

DIRECTIONS: Answer the following questions. Write your answers in complete sentences.

5. Store 3 claims they have shoes to fit any budget, since they have the largest range of prices. Look at the data for Store 3. Do you agree they have the best variety of prices? Explain.

_____

_____

_____

6. Which store has the lowest average price?

_____

7. If you wanted to find the store with the best variety of low-priced shoes, which would you choose? Which "middle number" could help you make this decision?

_____

STOP

Name _____ Date _____

| 10B.1 |

Gathering and Communicating Data

DIRECTIONS: Gina asked 250 students about their favorite types of restaurants. Her results are shown in the chart below. Use the chart to answer the questions.

Restaurant Type	Number
Italian	85
Bar & Grill	32
Mexican	45
Fast Food	70
Chinese	18

1. Each tick mark on the vertical axis in the chart below represents _____ people. Put a scale on the vertical axis.

2. Label the vertical axis.

3. What is the range of the data? _____

4. Complete the bar graph, using the data from the table.

Restaurant Preferences

Italian   Bar & Grill   Mexican   Fast Food   Chinese

5. How do you think Gina's data would have been different if she had asked people about their favorite restaurants as they were going into a local Italian diner? Explain.

_____

_____

 STOP

Name _____   Date _____

Collect, Organize, and
Analyze Data

Making Predictions

DIRECTIONS: Choose the best answer.

1. If all these chips were put into a bag, what is the probability that you would pick a chip with a letter that comes before M in the alphabet?

   Ⓐ $\frac{3}{5}$

   Ⓑ $\frac{3}{8}$

   Ⓒ $\frac{5}{3}$

   Ⓓ $\frac{5}{8}$

2. For the above chips, what is the probability that you would pick a chip with a vowel?

   Ⓕ $\frac{1}{7}$

   Ⓖ $\frac{1}{8}$

   Ⓗ $\frac{7}{1}$

   Ⓙ $\frac{8}{1}$

3. Which spinner would give you the best chance of landing on the number 2?

   Ⓐ [spinner: 1 2 / 4 3]

   Ⓑ [spinner: 1 2 / 2 3]

   Ⓒ [spinner: 1 2 / 3 3]

   Ⓓ [spinner: 1 2 / 3 1]

4. Which spinner would give you the best chance of landing on the number 4?

   Ⓕ [spinner: 1 2 / 4 3]

   Ⓖ [spinner: 1 2 / 2 3]

   Ⓗ [spinner: 1 2 / 3 3]

   Ⓙ [spinner: 1 2 / 3 1]

5. A bag of jellybeans contains 5 cherry jellybeans, 3 licorice jellybeans, 6 lime jellybeans, and 6 lemon jellybeans. When randomly pulling a jellybean from the bag, which two colors are you equally likely to pick?

   Ⓐ cherry and licorice

   Ⓑ licorice and lime

   Ⓒ lime and lemon

   Ⓓ cherry and lime

6. Carol wants a cherry jellybean. Without looking, she reaches into the bag and grabs a lime jellybean. She puts the jellybean back in the bag. Again, she randomly chooses a jellybean. How does her chance of getting a cherry jellybean on the second grab compare to her first grab?

   Ⓕ better

   Ⓖ worse

   Ⓗ same

   Ⓙ Not Here

STOP

Mathematics
10C.1

Listing Possible Outcomes

Collect, Organize, and
Analyze Data

DIRECTIONS: Choose the best answer.

 Clue Choose "Not Here" only if you are sure the right answer is not one of the choices. Look for key words, numbers, and figures in each problem, and be sure you perform the correct operation.

1. **There are 10 silver earrings and 10 gold earrings in a drawer. Cheryl reaches into her jewelry box without looking. What is the probability that she will pick a gold earring?**

   (A) $\frac{1}{2}$

   (B) $\frac{1}{3}$

   (C) $\frac{1}{4}$

   (D) Not Here

2. **A group of teachers are ordering sandwiches from the deli. They can choose ham, beef, turkey, or bologna on white bread, wheat bread, or rye bread. How many different meat and bread combinations are possible?**

   (F) 12

   (G) 16

   (H) 7

   (J) Not Here

3. **Elliott spun the arrow on a spinner 30 times. The results are shown in the table. Which of these spinners did Elliott most likely spin?**

Diamond	Heart	Spade	Total Spins
11	10	9	30

   (A)   (B)   (C)   (D)

4. **A snack food company makes chewy fruit shapes of lions, monkeys, elephants, and giraffes in red, green, purple, and yellow. They put the same number of each kind in a package. How many different outcomes are there?**

   (F) 4

   (G) 8

   (H) 16

   (J) Not Here

DIRECTIONS: For questions 5 and 6, draw a tree diagram to show all the outcomes.

5. **Draw the diagram for question 2.**

6. **A new car can be ordered in black, red, or tan. You may also choose leather or fabric seats. Show the outcomes.**

STOP

Mathematics

10C.2

Probable Outcomes

DIRECTIONS: For questions 1–8, write a **1** in the blank if the probability is certain; write a **0** if the probability is impossible; for other probabilities, write **NA.**

1. **A bag contains 10 nickels, 7 dimes, and 6 quarters. If you reach into the bag and take out one coin, what is the probability that the coin will be colored silver?** _____

2. **A bag contains 10 nickels, 7 dimes, and 6 quarters. If you reach into the bag and take out one coin, what is the probability that you will take a nickel?** _____

3. **A bag contains 10 nickels, 7 dimes, and 6 quarters. If you reach into the bag and take out one coin, what is the probability that the coin will be worth 50 cents?** _____

DIRECTIONS: Look at the spinner. What is the probability the arrow will land on

4. **an even number?** _____

5. **a 3?** _____

6. **a number smaller than 9?** _____

7. **a number larger than 2?** _____

8. **a single-digit number?** _____

Mathematics

10C.3

Expressing Probabilities

DIRECTIONS: Choose the best answer.

For questions 1–4, suppose you wrote the word *vacation* on a strip of paper and cut the paper into pieces with one letter per piece. If you put the pieces into a hat and pulled out one piece without looking, determine the probability of each situation.

1. **What is the probability that you would pick out the letter A?**
   - (A) 1 out of 8
   - (B) 2 out of 8
   - (C) 4 out of 5
   - (D) 2 out of 7

2. **Without returning the A to the hat, what is the probability that you would pick out the letter C?**
   - (F) 1 out of 8
   - (G) 1 out of 7
   - (H) 2 out of 8
   - (J) 1 out of 6

3. **Without returning the A or the C to the hat, what is the probability of picking a vowel?**
   - (A) 4 out of 8
   - (B) 3 out of 7
   - (C) 3 out of 5
   - (D) 3 out of 6

4. **Given the original word, what is the probability of picking a consonant?**
   - (F) 1 out of 8
   - (G) 4 out of 8
   - (H) 2 out of 8
   - (J) 4 out of 6

There are ten white tennis balls and ten green tennis balls in a box. Tony reaches into the box without looking.

5. **What is the probability that he will pick a white ball?**
   - (A) $\frac{1}{10}$
   - (B) $\frac{1}{2}$
   - (C) $\frac{1}{20}$
   - (D) $\frac{1}{5}$

6. **What is the probability that he will pick a green ball?**
   - (F) $\frac{1}{10}$
   - (G) $\frac{1}{20}$
   - (H) $\frac{1}{5}$
   - (J) $\frac{1}{2}$

7. **Tony picks a white ball. He returns it to the box. He wants another white ball. What is the probability that he will pick a white ball from the box on the next try?**
   - (A) $\frac{9}{16}$
   - (B) $\frac{1}{19}$
   - (C) $\frac{1}{5}$
   - (D) $\frac{1}{2}$

STOP

192

Name _____   Date _____

Mathematics

10C.4

Predicting and Testing Outcomes

DIRECTIONS: Think about rolling two six-sided dice. Which sum(s) are you most likely to roll? Least likely to roll? Complete the following activity to find out.

Predict answers to questions 1–7. Then, make a probability chart by following these directions. Make three columns on a piece of paper. The first column lists the sums 2 through 12. The second column is all possible combinations of dice pairs that will make the sums 2 through 12. Next, count the number of different ways you found the sum. Write this number in a "# of ways" column. You should find a total of 36 different pair combinations. Once you have completed the chart, answer the questions again. How many of your predictions were correct?

1. **Which sum is most likely to occur?**

   _____

   _____

2. **Which sums are least likely to occur?**

   _____

   _____

3. **Which sums have a chance of happening (meaning there are 5 possible ways to make the sum out of 36 total combinations)?**

   _____

4. **What is the probability of rolling a sum of 9?**

   _____

   _____

5. **What is the probability of rolling a sum of 10 or a sum of 5?**

   _____

   _____

6. **In many games, rolling doubles allows you to take another turn. How many different ways can you roll doubles?**

   _____

   _____

7. **What is the probability of rolling doubles?**

   _____

   _____

STOP

Mathematics

10

For pages 183–193

Mini-Test 5

Collect, Organize, and
Analyze Data

DIRECTIONS: Choose the best answer.

1. **What is the least favorite pet in Ms. Paice's class?**

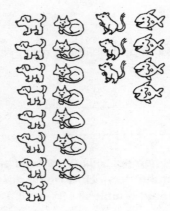

(A) dog

(B) cat

(C) gerbil

(D) fish

2. **If each** 🙂 **stands for 3 people, how would you show 12 people?**

(F) 🙂 🙂

(G) 🙂 🙂 🙂 🙂

(H) 🙂 🙂 🙂 🙂 🙂

(J) None of these

3. **What is the range of this data?**

31, 54, 34, 31, 56

(A) 31

(B) 54

(C) 56

(D) 25

DIRECTIONS: Use the following information for questions 4–6. A bag contains 7 red marbles, 5 green marbles, 3 white marbles, and 2 gold marbles.

4. **If you reach into the bag without looking, what is the probability of picking a red marble?**

(F) $\frac{7}{10}$

(G) $\frac{7}{17}$

(H) $\frac{7}{8}$

(J) $\frac{7}{9}$

5. **What is the probability of picking a gold marble?**

(A) $\frac{2}{17}$

(B) $\frac{2}{7}$

(C) $\frac{2}{5}$

(D) $\frac{2}{3}$

6. **What is the probability of picking a green marble?**

(F) $\frac{5}{7}$

(G) $\frac{5}{5}$

(H) $\frac{5}{15}$

(J) $\frac{5}{17}$

STOP

How Am I Doing?

Mini-Test 1	9–10 answers correct	**Great Job!** Move on to the section test on page 197.
	6–8 answers correct	**You're almost there!** But you still need a little practice. Review practice pages 116–133 before moving on to the section test on page 197.
Page 134 **Number Correct**	0–5 answers correct	**Oops!** Time to review what you have learned and try again. Review the practice section on pages 116–133. Then retake the test on page 134. Now move on to the section test on page 197.
Mini-Test 2	7–8 answers correct	**Awesome!** Move on to the section test on page 197.
	5–6 answers correct	**You're almost there!** But you still need a little practice. Review practice pages 136–145 before moving on to the section test on page 197.
Page 146 **Number Correct**	0–4 answers correct	**Oops!** Time to review what you have learned and try again. Review the practice section on pages 136–145. Then retake the test on page 146. Now move on to the section test on page 197.
Mini-Test 3	6 answers correct	**Great Job!** Move on to the section test on page 197.
	4–5 answers correct	**You're almost there!** But you still need a little practice. Review practice pages 148–160 before moving on to the section test on page 197.
Page 161 **Number Correct**	0–3 answers correct	**Oops!** Time to review what you have learned and try again. Review the practice section on pages 148–160. Then retake the test on page 161. Now move on to the section test on page 197.

How Am I Doing?

Mini-Test 4 Page 181 **Number Correct**	**6** answers correct	**Awesome!** Move on to the section test on page 197.
	4–5 answers correct	**You're almost there!** But you still need a little practice. Review practice pages 164–180 before moving on to the section test on page 197.
	0–3 answers correct	**Oops!** Time to review what you have learned and try again. Review the practice section on pages 164–180. Then retake the test on page 181. Now move on to the section test on page 197.
Mini-Test 5 Page 194 **Number Correct**	**6** answers correct	**Great Job!** Move on to the section test on page 197.
	4–5 answers correct	**You're almost there!** But you still need a little practice. Review practice pages 183–193 before moving on to the section test on page 197.
	0–3 answers correct	**Oops!** Time to review what you have learned and try again. Review the practice section on pages 183–193. Then retake the test on page 194. Now move on to the section test on page 197.

Name _____   Date _____

Final Mathematics Test
for pages 115–194

DIRECTIONS: Choose the best answer.

1. Which group of decimals is ordered from least to greatest?

    (A) 3.332, 3.321, 3.295, 3.287, 3.111

    (B) 3.424, 3.425, 3.339, 3.383, 3.214

    (C) 3.109, 3.107, 3.278, 3.229, 3.344

    (D) 3.132, 3.234, 3.262, 3.391, 3.406

2. Which of the following is not equivalent to the shaded portion of the figure?

    (F) $\frac{1}{3}$

    (G) $\frac{4}{8}$

    (H) $\frac{12}{36}$

    (J) $\frac{37}{111}$

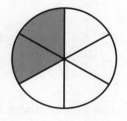

3. Cole and Jenny split a candy bar. Cole ate $\frac{3}{16}$ and Jenny ate $\frac{11}{16}$. Who ate more? Did they eat the whole candy bar?

    (A) Cole, yes

    (B) Jenny, yes

    (C) Cole, no

    (D) Jenny, no

4. It took Scott $\frac{3}{6}$ of an hour to get home. What is the decimal equivalent of $\frac{3}{6}$?

    (F) 0.5

    (G) 0.36

    (H) 2.0

    (J) Not Here

5. Myrtle and Doris collect stamps. Myrtle has 423 stamps and Doris has 519. How many stamps do both girls have?

    (A) 96

    (B) 942

    (C) 1,000

    (D) 100

6. A machine can produce 98 parts in one hour. How many parts could it produce in 72 hours?

    (F) 170

    (G) 26

    (H) 196

    (J) 7,056

7. Lucinda has 59 cents to buy pencils that cost 14 cents each. How many pencils can she buy?

    (A) 826

    (B) 45

    (C) 73

    (D) 4

8. Write 38 as the product of its prime factors by using exponents.

    (F) $4^2 \times 14$

    (G) $3^2 \times 8$

    (H) $2^2 \times 14$

    (J) $2^1 \times 19$

9. Which of these is a prime number?

    (A) 5

    (B) 9

    (C) 15

    (D) 21

GO →

10. Yesterday $\frac{3}{8}$ inch of rain fell. Today $\frac{5}{8}$ inch of rain fell. How much rain fell during the two days?

　F 1 inch

　G $\frac{2}{8}$ inch

　H 8 inches

　J $\frac{8}{16}$ inch

11. I am a number. I am the year of Columbus' famous voyage rounded to the nearest 1,000. What number am I?

　A 1000

　B 1400

　C 1492

　D 1500

12. The figure below is a sketch showing the cafeteria at Lincoln School. If you walked completely around the cafeteria, about how far would you go?

　F 100 ft

　G 80 ft

　H 120 ft

　J 400 ft

20 ft

13. Each column in the number pattern below equals 21. What numbers are missing?

3	5	2	1	6
2	7	8	9	1
9	8	4	6	7
	1	7		7

　A 6 and 8

　B 7 and 5

　C 1 and 7

　D 4 and 3

14. Look at the chart. Which of the following is the most likely time of sunrise on March 4?

Date	Time of Sunrise
March 1	6:39 A.M.
March 2	6:36 A.M.
March 3	6:33 A.M.
March 4	

　F 6:33 A.M.

　G 6:30 A.M.

　H 6:27 A.M.

　J Not Here

15. Which factors are represented by the figure?

　A 3×5

　B 6×2

　C 5×2

　D 3×6

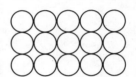

16. The school district had 8,927 students. Which of these is the expanded numeral for 8,927?

　F $89 + 27$

　G $800 + 900 + 200 + 7$

　H $9,000 + 800 + 20 + 7$

　J $8,000 + 900 + 20 + 7$

17. If sides a and c are parallel, which of the following is not true about sides b and d?

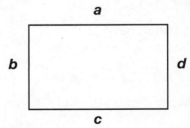

　A They are parallel.

　B They are equal in length.

　C They are perpendicular.

　D They are congruent.

GO

18. How many faces does the shape have?

- (F) 5
- (G) 6
- (H) 7
- (J) 8

DIRECTIONS: Use the graph for question 19.

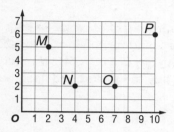

19. In the graph above, which point is located at (4, 2)?

- (A) P
- (B) O
- (C) N
- (D) M

DIRECTIONS: Use the bar graph for question 20.

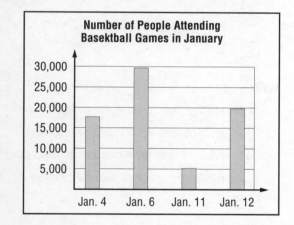

20. A snowstorm prevented many people from going to a basketball game in January. Use the graph above to determine on which date the storm occurred

- (F) Jan. 12
- (G) Jan. 4
- (H) Jan. 11
- (J) Jan. 6

21. What is the volume of this figure?

- (A) 150 cubic units
- (B) 100 cubic units
- (C) 53 cubic units
- (D) 50 cubic units

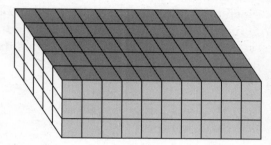

22. Jeremiah has a photograph that measures 5" × 7". He wants to frame the photograph using a 3-inch mat. What size picture frame will Jeremiah need to accommodate the photograph and mat?

- (F) 5" × 7"
- (G) 8" × 10"
- (H) 3" × 5"
- (J) 11" × 13"

23. A football is 11 inches in length. How many footballs would have to be placed end to end to equal more than 1 yard?

- (A) 1
- (B) 2
- (C) 3
- (D) 4

24. Five students were surveyed about their favorite meal in the cafeteria. Three of them said they liked pizza. What fraction shows the portion of students who liked pizza?

- (F) $\frac{5}{3}$
- (G) $\frac{3}{5}$
- (H) $\frac{2}{5}$
- (J) Not Here

GO

25. Timmy flips a coin 10 times and gets 8 heads and 2 tails. What would he expect the next flip to result in?

(A) heads

(B) tails

26. On a baseball diamond, it is 90 feet between each base, and there are four bases. Suppose a runner hits a double and has reached second base. How much farther does the runner have to go to reach home?

(F) 90 ft

(G) 180 ft

(H) 270 ft

(J) 360 ft

27. The Spanish Club wants to buy a set of instructional videos. Each video costs $12.50. What information will they need to determine how much money they must raise to buy the entire set of videos?

(A) the number of students in the school

(B) how long each video is

(C) the number of videos in the set

(D) how many students there are in the Spanish Club

28. Natasha is building her strength for the swimming season. She can now lift 75 pounds. She wants to increase the weight she can lift by 5 pounds a week for 6 weeks. At the end of 6 weeks, how much weight will she be able to lift?

(F) 105 pounds

(G) 30 pounds

(H) 92 pounds

(J) 80 pounds

29. An auto mechanic earns $19 an hour. She works 8 hours a day. Which number sentence shows how to find how much she earns in a day?

(A) $19 + 8 = \blacksquare$

(B) $19 - 8 = \blacksquare$

(C) $19 \times 8 = \blacksquare$

(D) $19 \div 8 = \blacksquare$

30. A waterproof jacket costs $49.95. The cold-weather lining for the jacket is $22.50 and a matching hat is $12.75. How much would it cost to buy the jacket and liner, but not the hat?

(F) $85.20

(G) $72.45

(H) $61.45

(J) $62.70

31. What value does b have to make both equations true?

$b - 7 = 15; 2 \times 11 = b$

(A) 85

(B) 12

(C) 21

(D) 22

32. Which of these rules is correct?

(F) Half of any even number is odd.

(G) Half of any even number is even.

(H) All odd numbers can be divided by 3.

(J) All even numbers can be divided by 2.

STOP

Name _____ Date _____

Mathematics Test
Answer Sheet

1. (A) (B) (C) (D)
2. (F) (G) (H) (J)
3. (A) (B) (C) (D)
4. (F) (G) (H) (J)
5. (A) (B) (C) (D)
6. (F) (G) (H) (J)
7. (A) (B) (C) (D)
8. (F) (G) (H) (J)
9. (A) (B) (C) (D)
10. (F) (G) (H) (J)

11. (A) (B) (C) (D)
12. (F) (G) (H) (J)
13. (A) (B) (C) (D)
14. (F) (G) (H) (J)
15. (A) (B) (C) (D)
16. (F) (G) (H) (J)
17. (A) (B) (C) (D)
18. (F) (G) (H) (J)
19. (A) (B) (C) (D)
20. (F) (G) (H) (J)

21. (A) (B) (C) (D)
22. (F) (G) (H) (J)
23. (A) (B) (C) (D)
24. (F) (G) (H) (J)
25. (A) (B)
26. (F) (G) (H) (J)
27. (A) (B) (C) (D)
28. (F) (G) (H) (J)
29. (A) (B) (C) (D)
30. (F) (G) (H) (J)

31. (A) (B) (C) (D)
32. (F) (G) (H) (J)

Answer Key

Page 8
1. what you spend your money on
2. items you subtract from your income
3. items you add to your income
4. relationship between debits and credits; the amount you have available to spend

Page 9
1. C
2. F
3. A
4. J
5. C
6. F
7. B
8. H
9. again
10. not
11. can be
12. a person who
13. being
14. after

Page 10
1. week
2. sale
3. meet
4. blew
5. lovely, good-looking, beautiful
6. blazing, smoking, burning
7. ugly, homely, bad-looking
8. cold, chilly, frigid
9. A
10. H
11. B
12. G
13. D
14. F

Page 11
1. B
2. J
3. D
4. G
5. A

Page 12
1. thrifty
2. energetic
3. smell
4. slender
5. timid
6. snickered
7. gossip
8. credulous

Page 13
1. D
2. G
3. D
4. F
5. C
6. J
7. D

Page 14
1. D
2. F
3. H
4. A
5. G
6. B
7. C
8. E

Page 15
1. D
2. H
3. A
4. G
5. A

Page 16
1. B
2. G
3. A
4. F
5. B

Page 17 Mini-Test 1
1. B
2. F
3. A
4. J
5. B
6. F
7. C
8. H
9. A

Page 19
1. A
2. J
3. C
4. J
5. D
6. H

Page 20
1. B
2. H

Pages 21–22
1. B
2. J
3. C
4. H
5. A
6. J
7. D

Page 23
1. ancient Rome
2. false
3. false
4. C

Pages 24–25
1. C
2. H
3. C
4. J
5. B
6. G
7. C

Pages 26–27
1. 1914
2. the United States
3. Isthmus
4. Panama
5. Atlantic
6. Pacific
7. to link the Atlantic and Pacific Oceans
8. disease
9. excavate earth to clear passages
10. build a dam across the Chagres River
11. build the series of locks
12. cost $380 million
13. runs 50 miles across the Isthmus of Panama
14. water in the canal is controlled by three sets of locks
15. The Republic of Panama—Today has responsibility for administration, upkeep, and maintenance of the canal.
16. United States—Built the canal in 1907–1914; operated the canal prior to 2000.
17. 1903—Gave the U.S. permission to build and operate the canal.
18. 1977—Transferred the responsibility for administration, upkeep, and maintenance of the canal to the Republic of Panama.

Pages 28–29

1. Color signals of red, blue, and green are added to the video signals.
2. The camera changes the light waves into electronic signals; video is produced.
3. The first television system was made.
4. Philo Farnsworth experiments with an idea to send pictures and sound through the air.
5. Television is invented.
6. Television has become one of the world's most important forms of communication, allowing people instant access to current events.
7. Electronic signals from the scene being televised are passed through the air.
8. The stage is set for the invention of television.
9. Electric signals are unscrambled and changed into the original light and sound waves.
10. Televisions have wider screens and clearer pictures.

Pages 30–31

1. 1783—first real balloon flight (with animals); first people to fly in a balloon; first flight in a hydrogen balloon; 1784—ballooning became popular in France; 1863—a balloon corps flew for the Union Army.
2. C
3. J
4. A
5. T
6. F
7. F
8. T
9. T
10. F

Page 32

1. B
2. F
3. D
4. J
5. B

Page 33 Mini-Test 2

1. B
2. H
3. D
4. F

Page 35

1. Answers will vary. Cross-country skiing is easier to do because it does not require a special location.
2. Answers will vary. Downhill skiing is most expensive because it must be done at a ski resort.

Page 36

Answers will vary. Questions should be open-ended and related to the text.

Pages 37–38

1. You could tell whether the elephants prefer to use their right or left tusks. The tusks they use most often would be shorter. You could also tell whether the elephant lives in the savanna (longer, curved tusks) or the forest (shorter tusks).
2. The elephant might have become extinct if hunters had kept killing it for its tusks.
3. A poacher is someone who kills an animal illegally. A poacher breaks the law to earn money from an elephant's tusks.
4. Poachers had to find other ways to make money once the ivory trade was illegal. Poachers also might have decided to disobey the law and continue to hunt elephants for their tusks.
5. If ivory trade was made legal again, elephants might be at risk. People might continue to kill elephants for their tusks. Then there might be very few elephants left in the world.
6. Answers will vary. To continue to protect the elephants, the ivory trade should stay illegal. We should help develop opportunities in poor countries so people have better ways to earn money.

Pages 39–40

Li Lui
house—apartment building
where they live—city: Beijing
where they live—country: China
TV show—cartoons
what they like—food: shrimp chips
what they like—drink: soda
uniform—blue warm-up suit
school—favorite subject: art, Chinese
school—least favorite subject: math

Yena
house—one-floor house
where they live—city: Accra
where they live—country: Ghana
TV show—cartoons
what they like—food: plantains
what they like—drink: fruit juice
uniform—brown dress, yellow shirt
school—favorite subject: science
school—least favorite subject: French

Page 41
1. Ben Hanson wrote the first passage; the second passage appeared in the newspaper.
2. Answers will vary. Possible answers: Both passages tell that (a) Ben missed the word *cannibal;* (b) a girl named Rebecca won the spelling bee; and (c) Ben won a dictionary.
3. Answers will vary. Possible answers: (a) only the diary entry tells how nervous Ben was at first; (b) only the newspaper entry tells Rebecca's last name; (c) only the newspaper article tells how many words Ben spelled correctly.

Page 42
1. B
2. J
3. C
4. F
5. C

Pages 43–44
1. A
2. F
3. B
4. 2,150
5. 1,800
6. 25, 15
7. stones
8. 100, 200
9. 40
10. food, water, supplies

11. Answers will vary. One possible answer could suggest that the Great Wall could not withstand attacks from large enemy forces, only from small forces.

Pages 45–46
1. M, S, S, S
2. Sollie is athletic and graceful but sinks in the water and was being thrown around behind the boat when he forgot to let go of the rope.
3. B
4. Answers will vary. One possible answer: like a dolphin racing down the coast.
5. Sollie is a seal, sleek and smooth in the water.

Page 47
1. Answers may vary but should generally revolve around an explanation of why Easter Island is a source of mystery.
2. Answers may vary. Two possible answers are (1) the drawings emphasize the strange, eerie nature of the statues and (2) the map shows the remoteness of Easter Island, which contributes to its mystery.

Page 48
1. 1994; it allowed listeners to hear sounds almost at the moment they were said.
2. after
3. Eisenhower sets up an agency for technology.
4. A computer network is planned.
5. 8
6. 50 million

Page 49
1. passages A, B, C, and E
2. passage F
3. passage B
4. passage C
5. passage A

Pages 50–51
Mini-Test 3
1. Gustave Eiffel believed the Eiffel Tower could be completed in two years. No one else shared his opinion.
2. Yes. The Eiffel Tower can be judged a financial success because it was built for less money than Eiffel thought it would cost. Also, no risk was involved because Eiffel agreed to provide the money himself if the tower was not a financial success.
3. The facts help the reader understand the size of the tower. The facts show the immense effort required to build such a large structure.

4. Answers will vary.
5. Gustave Eiffel was a success in life because he was a master builder. He was famous for his work with iron. He completed on time and for less money than expected what was then the tallest structure in the world. His tower still stands today, proving the importance of his work.
6. Answers will vary.

Page 53
1. D
2. The story is about an animal and has a moral.
3. A fable is usually about animals. A fable includes details about a moral or character lesson.

Pages 54–55
1. Answers may vary but should take into account the setting and language used by the characters. A possible answer is in medieval England.
2. Answers may vary. Possible answers: The dialect is old-fashioned, belonging to a different time than today. Characters may be dressed in royal-looking garb.

3. Rowan's pony is "little larger than a dog." She is referred to as a "child."
4. He is described as being "evil" and having a "huge form." When he speaks, the story says "he roared." One of the horsemen trembles in his presence.
5. Answers will vary. One possible answer: The language and clothing of the characters would be different. They would perhaps be driving cars rather than riding horses. Their names might be different.

Pages 56–57
1. A. squirrel, adoring; B. rabbit, practical
2. A squirrel wants a rabbit to leave her burrow, marry him, and live with him in the trees, but she refuses.
3. Answers will vary. One possible answer is "the value of knowing where you belong."
4. hopeful, lovesick
5. annoyed, realistic
6. The squirrel describes his home as far above the rabbit's home in the warren.

7. The rabbit lives in a sheltered hollow, from which she can reach gardens with carrots and cabbages. The squirrel lives up in the trees.

Pages 58–59
1. Robin is polite.
   A. She says "thank you."
   B. She brings a hostess gift.
2. Sheila is greedy.
   A. She grabs the candy.
   B. She asks for milk.
3. Tamiko is fearful.
   A. She wants to call her parents.
   B. She brought a flashlight and a teddy bear.
4. Paula is rude.
   A. She asks if her boyfriend can come over.
   B. She rolls her eyes.
5. Ted is mischievous.
   A. He is wearing a mask.
   B. He plans to scare the girls.

Page 60
1. B
2. H
3. D
4. H

Pages 61–62
Setting—The Kingdom of Tess
Main Character—The old man with the original dress.
Problem—Beasts, birdies, and boys ate his "clothes."
Main Events—He dressed up. He went for a walk. His clothes were eaten. He ran home.
Craziest Moment—Answers will vary.
Solution—He will not dress in a similar way again.

Page 63
Hibernation

Main purpose is to inform

Organized according to the purpose the authors wish to achieve (steps to achieve a goal; explain why something happens; attempt to make an argument; etc.)

Waterland

Made up or fantasized

Main purpose is to entertain

Organized into setting, characters, problem, goal, events, and resolution

Page 64 Mini-Test 4
1. Phil, Mary Ann, Susy
2. Phil
3. One afternoon in March, on a sidewalk in the city
4. A
5. G

Page 66
Answers will vary. A possible alternate ending:

"I don't suppose you'd like to go to the movies with me this Saturday?" Alex whispered to CeCe. But before she got a chance to answer, the teacher looked up. "Alex and CeCe. No talking. Save it for after class."

Alex and CeCe smiled shyly at each other. *Right after class, I'm going to ask her,* thought Alex. *I'll have to remember to thank my dad.*

Page 67
1. C
2. F
3. D
4. H

Pages 68–69

Theo
personality—
   hardworking,
   disciplined
feelings before race—
   nervous
uniform color—red and
   white
team members—
   seventeen
main event—400-meter
   dash
other events—high jump

Carl
personality—friendly,
   determined
feelings before race—
   calm
uniform color—none
   (gray T-shirt)
team members—
   no team
main event—400-meter
   dash
other events—none

1. 22
2. uniforms from all
   the schools
3. since early March
4. May
5. warm, sunny
6. 8

Page 70

1. why the sun and
   moon appear in
   the sky
2. why porcupines
   have four claws
   on each foot
3. One Who Walks
   All Over the Sky
   and Walking
   About Early;
   Porcupine and
   Beaver
4. They both cared
   about their
   environment
   and wanted to
   change it.

Page 71

1. D
2. F
3. B
4. J

Page 72

1. textbook
2. newspaper
3. biography
4. instruction
   manual
5. A
6. G

Page 73

1. B
2. J
3. B
4. Answers may
   vary. Possible
   answer: I love
   to watch her
   gallop around
   the pasture. She
   runs like the wind
   and looks so
   carefree. I hope
   I'll see her run
   that way again.

Page 74 Mini-Test 5

1. A
2. G
3. Answers will vary.
   A possible
   answer might
   describe Misha
   and his music
   teacher meeting
   after the concert
   and happily
   discussing
   Misha's
   performance.

Pages 77–80
Final Reading Test

1. C
2. F
3. D
4. F
5. A
6. G
7. B
8. J
9. A
10. F
11. D
12. H
13. A
14. J
15. A
16. G
17. A
18. J
19. C
20. F
21. B
22. H
23. A
24. F
25. D
26. G
27. A
28. F
29. D
30. J
31. D

Page 83

1. IN
   You are on a
   deserted island:
   no town, no
   people—just you
   and those crazy,
   noisy seagulls.
   What are you
   going to do?
2. NONE
   Toward the castle
   she fled. She
   begged the
   gatekeeper for
   entrance. He was
   as deaf as a
   gargoyle. He did
   not hear her cries.
   Past the stone
   walls she
   scurried, the
   hounds in pursuit.

3. NONE
   Maggie bit her lip.
   No use crying
   about it. She
   pulled her math
   homework out of
   the sink and just
   stared at her little
   sister.
4. IN
   The music is
   playing those
   lovely Christmas
   tunes, but you're
   not listening. You
   can't. You have
   too many impor-
   tant things to
   plan. What should
   you buy for
   Teddie? Who
   should you invite
   to the party? And
   . . .
5. NONE
   I'm not proud of
   it. Really, I am
   not. But no
   teacher's ever
   gotten through to
   me. I guess I'm
   just not cut out to
   be a scholar.
6. EX
   Columbus stood
   on the deck of
   the ship. Land
   was on the
   horizon. Land!
   Not the edge of
   the world, not
   dragons to
   devour the ship,
   but the land that
   would make his
   fortune . . . his
   and Spain's.

7. EX
   <u>I think Mama forgot me. Otherwise, she would come and find me.</u> Oh, no! I've been bad! <u>Mama said not to go see the toys because I'd get lost.</u> Mama is going to be mad at me!

8. IM
   Do not stop until you reach the end of this story. <u>What you are about to read is so amazing that you simply must hear about it now.</u> So settle back and get ready for the most incredible tale you've ever heard.

9. and 10.
   Answers will vary. Students should include all four sentence types at least once in the paragraph.

Page 84
Answers will vary. In the first paragraph, students should describe a job they could do in the neighborhood. In the second paragraph, students should give two reasons why neighbors would choose them to do the job they chose. In the concluding paragraph, students should convince their neighbors to hire them.

Page 85
1. C
2. I can ride faster than you can. Let's race to the stop sign.
3. I'm thirsty. Does anyone have some bottled water?
4. We need to be careful on the bike trail. In-line skaters can appear fast.
5. C
6. I love the playground. It has great swings.
7. When I swing too high, I get sick. Do you?
8. C
9. This ride was fun. Let's do it again tomorrow.
10.–13. Students' answers will vary but they should correctly rewrite each fragment into a complete sentence.

Page 86
1. B
2. H
3. D

Page 87
1. C
2. H
3. B
4. G
5. A
6. H
7. D
8. J

Page 88
1. A
2. F
3. C
4. F
5. B
6. H

Page 89 Mini-Test 1
1. D
2. F
3. B
4. G
5. D
6. Answers will vary. Students should write about their favorite desserts and should include at least one interrogative or exclamatory sentence in their paragraphs.

Page 91
1. Answers will vary but should include three memorable experiences.
2. Answers will vary but should describe the students' chosen experiences.
3. Answers will vary but should describe the three most important things the students would want to relate about their chosen experiences.

Page 92
1. B
2. J
3. C
4. G

Page 93
1. C
2. G
3. D
4. F

Page 94
Answers will vary, but students' paragraphs should explain an activity using a logical order of directions and sufficient detail.

Page 95
Answers will vary, but students' directions should have the steps in a logical order, and the instructions should be clear. Students should make appropriate use of transition words between steps.

Pages 96–97
1. The main focus of this passage is Tara's lost science report and what she will do about it.
2. D
3. A
4. A
5. D
6. A
7. A
8. D
9. D
10. D
11. Answers will vary. Students should write their descriptions in complete sentences.
12. Answers will vary. Answers should include a well-developed sequence of events that happen in a logical order. Answers should be written in complete sentences.

Pages 98–99

1. in the box
2. at city hall
3. under the bag
4. for the library book
5. to the applause; of the crowd
6. to the girls' volleyball team
7. on the list
8. in the dishwater
9. in half; over the fence
10. to the class; with the best attendance
11.–18. Students' answers will vary but should include prepositional phrases appropriate for each sentence.
19. adjective
20. adjective
21. adverb
22. adjective
23. adverb
24. adjective
25. adverb
26. adjective
27. adjective
28. adjective
29. adjective
30. adjective
31. adverb
32. adverb
33. adjective
34. adjective
35. adverb
36. adverb
37. Students' paragraphs should provide detailed descriptions of their favorite places and should include a variety of adjectives and adverbs.

Page 100

Let's all get together and help the Junior Red Cross. There are lots of people needing the organization's help right now. They're sponsoring a clothing drive to help people caught in the recent flood. Women's dresses, men's shirts, and children's clothing are especially needed. If you've outgrown any clothing or have clothing you don't use, please bring it in. It'll help brighten someone's day!

Page 101 Mini-Test 2

1. B
2. J
3. C
4. H
5. C

Page 103

1. D
2. G
3. C
4. F
5. D

Page 104

Student's paragraph should give a detailed description of the funniest thing that has happened to him or her, an explanation of his or her favorite sport or game, and a convincing argument about making a class outing to a local amusement park.

Page 105

Student's letter should be written to a favorite book character and should tell why the character is admired. Letter should also include a description of what the student might have done in situations similar to those encountered by the character and either an invitation or a piece of advice.

Page 106

Student's essay should present personal views on a topic that has more than one side to it. Supporting details and a reasonable conclusion should be included.

Page 107 Mini-Test 3

Student's paragraph should describe his or her favorite way to spend a day. Student should provide plenty of details and words that express his or her feelings.

Pages 109–111
Final Writing Test

1. A
2. J
3. A
4. J
5. A
6. G
7. B
8. H
9. B
10. F
11. D
12. F
13. C
14. G
15. B
16. G
17. A
18. J
19. A

Page 115

1. B
2. J
3. A
4. H
5. B
6. F
7. C
8. H
9. D
10. G

Page 116

1. C
2. F
3. C
4. J
5. B
6. H

Page 117

1. C
2. J
3. A
4. H

Page 118

1. C
2. G
3. C
4. G

Page 119

1. C
2. G
3. porpoise: −2
   bird: 4
   eel: −9
   flag on sailboat: 3
   sea horse: −7
   octopus: −4
   clouds: 6
   jellyfish: −6
4. Circled items:
   porpoise, clouds,
   flag, sail of boat,
   buoy, bird
5. eel, jellyfish, octo-
   pus, porpoise,
   buoy, bird, clouds

Page 120

1. A
2. J
3. A
4. G
5. A
6. J

Page 121

1. $2 \times 3 \times 5 \times 7$
2. $2 \times 2 \times 11$
3. $2 \times 3 \times 5 \times 5 \times 7$

Page 122

1. B
2. J
3. D
4. G
5. A
6. H
7. C
8. H

Page 123

1. 90, 450, 725,
   6.64, .083
2. 900; 4,500; 7,250;
   66.4; .83
3. 9,000; 45,000;
   72,500; 664; 8.3
4. $194.50
5. $1,945
6. $19,450
7. .2, .763, 29.1,
   1.86, .004
8. .02, .0763, 2.91,
   .186, .0004
9. .002, .00763,
   .291, .0186,
   .00004

Page 124

1. C
2. J
3. D
4. G
5. C

Page 125

1. B
2. J
3. A
4. H
5. C
6. J
7. A
8. G

Page 126

1. D
2. F
3. C
4. F
5. A
6. H
7. A
8. H

Page 127

1. A
2. G
3. B
4. F
5. A

Page 128

1. Incorrect.
   Estimate:
   700 × 30 =
   21,000
   Exact: 21,315
2. Correct
3. Correct
4. Incorrect.
   Estimate:
   2,000 × 600 =
   1,200,000
   Exact: 1,496,060
5. Incorrect.
   Estimate:
   1,300,000 +
   100,000 =
   1,400,000
   Exact: 1,373,067
6. Correct
7. Incorrect.
   Estimate:
   500 × 700 =
   350,000
   Exact: 323,532
8. Incorrect.
   Estimate:
   400 + 8,000 =
   8,400
   Exact: 8,320

Pages 129–130

1. A
2. G
3. A
4. H
5. D
6. H
7. B
8. H
9. C
10. F
11. D
12. H
13. B
14. F
15. A
16. F
17. B

Page 131

1. Jose's mother
   should estimate
   the costs, add the
   tax, and round
   the number up.
   It's better to have
   too much money
   than not enough.
2. The clerk knows
   the prices and
   tax, so the
   amount will be
   exact.
3. To order carpet,
   Mr. Mason will
   need to know
   exactly how big
   the space is.
4. If you subtract
   the number on
   the odometer
   before the trip
   from the number
   after the trip, the
   answer will be
   exact.
5. The amount will
   vary because it is
   not measured
   exactly as it is
   poured from the
   bottle.
6. The amount of
   time will be an
   estimate because
   speed and condi-
   tions could vary.
7. The temperature
   will be an exact
   measure because
   of the use of a
   thermometer.
8. They should
   estimate how
   many pictures
   they want to take
   and buy enough
   to cover that
   rounded amount.
9. Rashawn has to
   buy the exact
   number of tickets
   because each
   person will need
   one.

Pages 132–133
1. C
2. J
3. B
4. F
5. D
6. G
7. A
8. $\frac{2}{3} = 66\%$
9. $\frac{1}{2} = 50\%$
10. $\frac{1}{4} = 25\%$
11. $\frac{1}{2} = 50\%$
12. $\frac{2}{10} = 20\%$
13. $\frac{1}{3} = 33\%$
14. $\frac{1}{4} = 25\%$
15. $\frac{2}{6} = 33\%$
16. $1 = 100\%$

Page 134 Mini-Test 1
1. A
2. H
3. D
4. F
5. D
6. H
7. D
8. F
9. C
10. J

Pages 136–137
1. A
2. G
3. A
4. G
5. B
6. G
7. B
8. G

Page 138
1. 13 centimeters
2. 1.25 inches
3. .25 mile
4. 4 meters
5. 20,000 feet
6. C
7. F
8. C
9. F

Page 139
1. D
2. A
3. H
4. I
5. B
6. C
7. G
8. F
9. E
10. L
11. kL
12. mL

Pages 140–141
1. C
2. F
3. 5
4. 6
5. 6
6. 5
7. 14
8. 9

Page 142
1. A
2. F
3. D
4. G
5. C
6. F
7. B
8. H

Page 143
1. D
2. G
3. perimeter: 30 cm
   area: 45 cm^2
4. perimeter: 24 in.
   area: 20 in^2
5. perimeter: 15 ft.
   area: 10.5 ft^2

Page 144
1. B
2. H
3. A
4. 9
5. 9
6. 9

Page 145

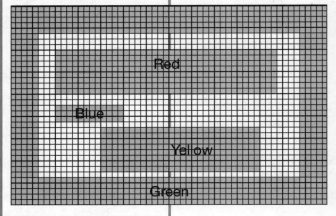

Page 146 Mini-Test 2
1. 21
2. 2
3. 40
4. C
5. F
6. D
7. J
8. C

Page 148
1. The star travels counterclockwise around the triangle. In the next three shapes, the star is in the left corner, right corner, and top.
2. The pattern is a dark pentagon followed by two shaded pentagons. The next three shapes: shaded pentagon, dark pentagon, shaded pentagon.
3. The pattern is eyes open, right wink, left wink. The next three shapes: right wink, left wink, eyes open.
4. 29, 36, 43

Page 149
1. 21, 23, 25
2. 0, 3, 6, 9, 12, 15
3. 3, 9, 15, 21, 27, 33
4. $y = x + 4$
5. $y = 4x$
6. $y = x - 2$
7. top row: 16; bottom row: 9, 24, 42; rule: subtract 13 from top row
8. top row: 25, 42; bottom row: 90, 46; rule: add 9 to top row
9. top row: 50; bottom row: 35, 17, 30; rule: divide top row numbers by 2

Page 150
1. C
2. J
3. D
4. G
5. A
6. J

Page 151
1. A
2. G
3. B
4. J

Page 152
1. D
2. F
3. C

Page 153
1. A
2. F
3. C
4. J
5. B
6. G

Pages 154–155
1. C
2. G
3. D
4. H
5. B
6. G
7. D
8. G
9. B
10. F
11. A
12. F

Pages 156–157
1.

Shape	1st	2nd	3rd	4th	5th	6th	7th	8th
Number of Tiles	1	3	6	10	15	21	28	36

2. The pattern grows by successive integers: +2, +3, +4, +5, +6, etc.
3. 55
4.

Number of Tables	1	2	3	4	5	6	7	8
Number of Guests	4	6	8	10	12	14	16	18

5. The number of guests increases by two for each table added.
6. 22
7.

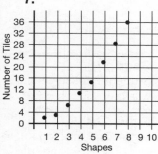

8.

9. Pattern B has higher values in the beginning. Pattern A has higher values at the end.
10. Pattern A begins growing gradually, but then gets steeper. Pattern B grows by the same amount each time.

Pages 158–159
1. B
2. G
3. C
4. G
5. A
6. J
7. A
8. G
9. A
10. G
11. D
12. F
13. C
14. H
15. A
16. G
17. C
18. H

Page 160
1. A
2. J
3. C
4. G
5. B
6. F

Page 161 Mini-Test 3
1. B
2. H
3. A
4. J
5. D
6. F

Page 164
1. D
2. G
3. A
4. J
5. B

Page 165
1. B
2. F
3. D
4. F
5. D
6. J
7. B
8. F

Page 166
1. A
2. H
3. C
4. G

Page 167
1. F = (2,6), L = (5,6), A = (5,4), G = (5,2)
2. B = (−2,2), O = (1,2), X = (1,−1), D = (−2,−1)
3. S = (2,−3), H = (2,−5), A = (−2,−5), P = (−2,−6), E = (−5,−6)
4. C

Page 168
1. start at town A; travel through towns B and D to reach town C.
2. 6 miles
3. 11 miles
4. 2 miles west, 5 miles north, 6 miles east, 3 miles south, 2 miles east, and 3 miles north
5. 3 miles north, 6 miles west, and 1 mile south

Page 169
1. yes
2. yes
3. yes
4. yes
5. no
6. no
7. yes
8. yes
9. yes
10. no
11. yes
12. no

Page 170
Answers will vary. Students should find at least two examples of a square, rectangle, circle, cone, cylinder, and sphere in their environment.

Page 171

1. Triangle

4. Square

2. Rectangle

5. Pyramid

3. Scalene triangle

6. Sphere

Page 172

1.

2.

3.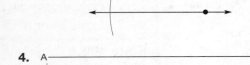

4. A ——————————— B

Page 173

1.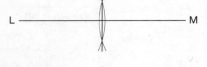

2.

3. O ——————————— R

Page 174
1. B
2. J
3. C
4. J
5. D

Page 175
1. congruent
2. congruent
3. congruent
4. similar
5. congruent
6. similar
7. congruent

Page 176
1. A
2. G
3. D

Page 177
1. B
2. F
3. C
4. J

Page 178
Students' tessellations will vary.

Page 179
1. The missing angle is 20°. Students' explanations may vary but should center around the fact that the sum of all three angles of a triangle equals 180°.
2. The missing angle is 128°. Students' explanations may vary but should center around the fact that the sum of all four angles of a triangle equals 360°.

3. The shape would be a cube. Students' explanations may vary but should center around the fact that the shape would have six sides of equal length.

Page 180
1. The result would be two squares. Students' measurements should confirm this answer by showing that two shapes each with four right angles and sides of equal length would result.
2. The result would be two right triangles. Students' measurements should confirm this answer by showing that two triangles each with an angle of 90° would result.

Page 181 Mini-Test 4
1. A
2. G
3. D
4. G
5. C
6. J
7. B

Pages 183–184

1.

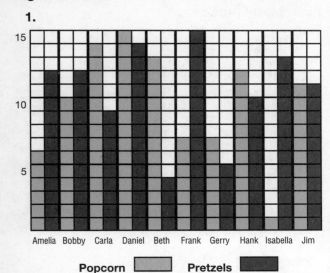

15
10
5

Amelia Bobby Carla Daniel Beth Frank Gerry Hank Isabella Jim

Popcorn ▢ **Pretzels** ▬

2.

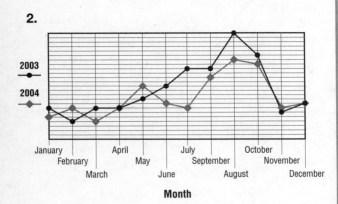

2003
2004

January February March April May June July September October November December
August

Month

3.

Test Scores (out of 40 pts)	
Stem	Leaf
2	5 6 8
3	0 2 2 4 5 5 7 8 9
4	0 0 0

Page 185

1.

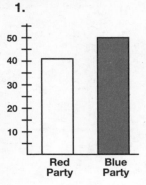

50
40
30
20
10

Red Party Blue Party

2.

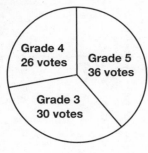

Grade 4 26 votes
Grade 5 36 votes
Grade 3 30 votes

Page 186

1. D
2. F
3. A
4. F
5. D
6. G

Page 187

1. Mean: $44.20; Median: $45; Mode: $45; Range: $50; Minimum value: $20; Maximum value: $70
2. Mean: $48; Median: $41; Mode: $35; Range: $55; Minimum value: $25; Maximum value: $80
3. Mean: $64.09; Median: $60; Mode: $85; Range: $80; Minimum value: $20; Maximum value: $100

4. Mean: $62.70; Median: $60; Mode: $60; Range: $56; Minimum value: $32; Maximum value: $88
5. Answers will vary. Students might agree because Store 3 has one of the least expensive pairs, as well as medium- and high-priced pairs. Other students might point out that Stores 1 and 2 offer a greater variety of inexpensive medium-priced shoes.
6. Store 1
7. Answers will vary. Store 2 is probably the best choice because it has the lowest median, indicating that half of the store's shoes are relatively inexpensive.

Page 188

1. 10
2. Number of People
3. 67
4.

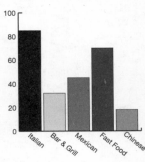

100
80
60
40
20
0

Italian Bar & Grill Mexican Fast Food Chinese

5. Answers will vary. Possible answer: Had Gina asked diners at an Italian restaurant about their favorite place to eat, she would probably have received more than 85 votes for Italian because people who are eating at an Italian restaurant probably enjoy Italian food.

Page 189
1. D
2. G
3. B
4. F
5. C
6. H

Page 190
1. A
2. F
3. B
4. H
5.

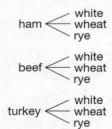

6.

Page 191
1. 1
2. NA
3. 0
4. 0
5. NA
6. NA
7. 1
8. 1

Page 192
1. B
2. G
3. D
4. G
5. B
6. J
7. D

Page 193
1. 7
2. 2, 12
3. 6, 8
4. $\frac{1}{9}$
5. $\frac{2}{9}$
6. 6
7. $\frac{1}{6}$

Page 194 Mini-Test 5
1. C
2. G
3. D
4. G
5. A
6. J

Pages 197–200
Final Mathematics Test
1. D
2. G
3. D
4. F
5. B
6. J
7. D
8. J
9. A
10. F
11. A
12. F
13. B
14. G
15. A
16. J
17. C
18. H
19. C
20. H
21. A
22. G
23. D
24. G
25. A
26. G
27. C
28. F
29. C
30. G
31. D
32. J

Notes

Notes